Thou Art That
A SKELETON KEY STUDY GUIDE

Thou Art That

A SKELETON KEY STUDY GUIDE

by

ANDREW GUREVICH

Copyright © 2023 Joseph Campbell Foundation

All rights reserved. No part of this publication may be reproduced, distributed, or transmitted in any form or by any means, including photocopying, recording, or other electronic or mechanical methods, without the prior written permission of the publisher, except in the case of brief quotations embodied in critical reviews and certain other noncommercial uses permitted by copyright law. For permission requests, please contact the Joseph Campbell Foundation's Rights and Permissions Manager at rights@jcf.org.

ISBN: 978-1-61178-041-3

Front cover image detail from fresco by Michelangelo of the Erythraean Sibyl from the Sistine Chapel, Vatican City.

Book design by *the*BookDesigners.

First printing, 2023

www.jcf.org

Contents

About *The Collected Works of Joseph Campbell* and the Joseph Campbell Foundation Skeleton Key Study Guide Series 1

How to Use This Study Guide 3

Skeleton Key Study Guide Introduction
by Andrew Gurevich 5

CHAPTER I
Metaphor and Religious Mystery 27

CHAPTER II
The Experience of Religious Mystery 45

CHAPTER III
The Religious Imagination
and the Rules of Traditional Theology. 63

CHAPTER IV
Mythogenesis. 83

CHAPTER V
Symbols of the Judeo-Christian Tradition 97

CHAPTER VI
Understanding the Symbols of Judeo-Christian Spirituality. . 115

CHAPTER VII
Question Period. 137

APPENDIX
A Discussion 157

Final Thoughts from Andrew Gurevich 175

About Joseph Campbell 181

About the Author. 183

About the Joseph Campbell Foundation 184

About
The Collected Works of Joseph Campbell
AND THE JOSEPH CAMPBELL FOUNDATION SKELETON KEY STUDY GUIDE SERIES

At his death in 1987, Joseph Campbell left a significant body of published work that explored his lifelong passion for myths and symbols from many cultures. He also left a large volume of unreleased work: uncollected articles, notes, letters, and diaries, as well as audio- and videotape recorded lectures.

The Joseph Campbell Foundation was founded in 1991 to preserve, promote, and perpetuate Campbell's work. The Foundation has undertaken to archive his papers and recordings in digital format, and to publish previously unavailable material and out-of-print works as *The Collected Works of Joseph Campbell*.

The Foundation is now also publishing this series of Skeleton Key Study Guides to accompany selected titles in the *Collected Works*. We intend study guides such as this one to provide entry points into Campbell's ideas for students and for others new to Campbell studies. We hope that Campbell's work and his way of working inspire you to bring new creativity, mythic awareness, and psychological depth to your own work, as they have already done for so many.

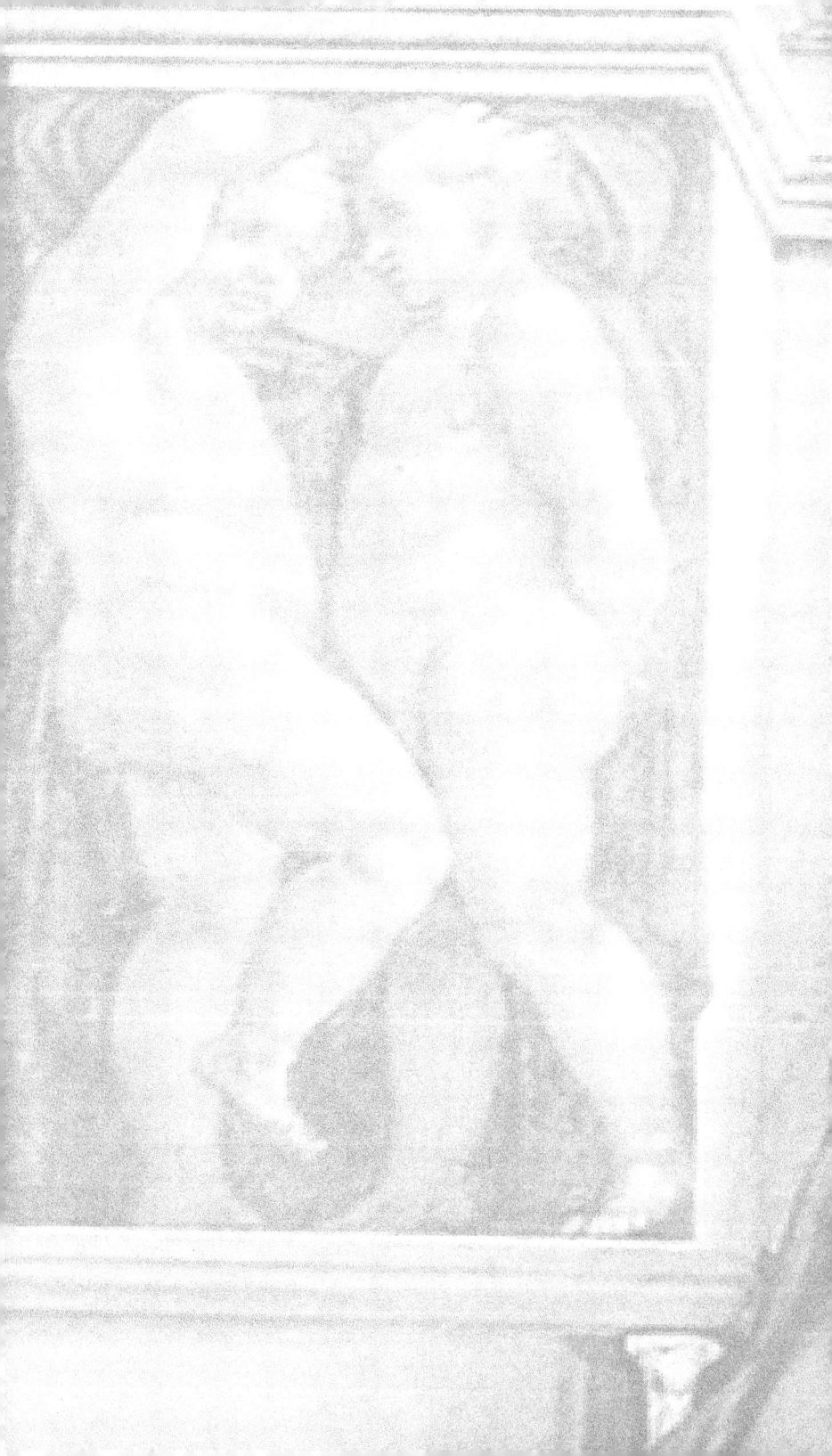

How to Use This Study Guide

A skeleton key can open many locks because it has been filed down to only the essentials. This study guide opens *Thou Art That: Transforming Religious Metaphor* the same way. Each chapter of the study guide focuses on a corresponding chapter in *Thou Art That*. In each chapter, you'll find a summary of the *Thou Art That* chapter, section by section, followed by points of interest in that chapter, as well as complementary reading lists. Chapters close with a selection of discussion questions, essay topics, and creative prompts. Our vision is that this study guide unlocks *Thou Art That* for you, whether you are new to the material or deepening your relationship with it.

CITATIONS FROM *THOU ART THAT*

Whenever this study guide quotes directly from *Thou Art That: Transforming Religious Metaphor*, the text includes footnotes that contain page numbers on which you can find the original citation. These page numbers refer to the edition published in 2001 by New World Library.

Campbell, Joseph. *Thou Art That: Transforming Religious Metaphor.* New World Library, 2001.

Skeleton Key Study Guide
Introduction by Andrew Gurevich

"What you are, basically, deep, deep down, far, far in, is simply the fabric and structure of existence itself."

—Alan Watts

"In the beginning there was Existence alone—One only, without a second. He, the One, thought to himself: Let me be many, let me grow forth. Thus out of himself he projected the universe, and having projected out of himself the universe, he entered into every being. All that is has its self in him alone. Of all things he is the subtle essence. He is the truth. He is the self. And that ... THOU ART THAT."

—*Chandogya Upanishad*[2]

All mythologies, according to Joseph Campbell, come to us through a specific culture and speak to us through the language and symbols of that culture. The notion is that the *moral* order in traditional mythologies is organically related to, or somehow emerges from within, the *cosmic* order. Thus, no discussion of the Absolute can occur without first rooting itself in place. No consideration of that which is *beyond time and space* can happen except *through* the lived experience of earth, sky, water, and flesh.

For example, salmon are extremely important to both the lifestyle and the spirituality of many Indigenous cultures, especially the tribes of the American Northwest Coast and the Columbia River. Like the buffalo, salmon are believed to willingly give themselves up as food to humans in many myths of the region.

The Indigenous cultures of the Pacific Northwest view the salmon as more than a simple food source, however. In their mythological lifeworlds, the salmon are symbols of perseverance, self-sacrifice, determination, regeneration, and prosperity. Therefore, they are considered sacred beings and hold a special position of honor and respect in the community.

The return of the fish to their spawning grounds is celebrated each year at the beginning of fishing season with special dances and "first return" ceremonies to show appreciation for the sacred sacrifice. This celebration and harvest are important aspects of Northwest Coast tribal life, as they also involve the transfer of traditional values from generation to generation. In other words, the salmon myths contain the potential to establish and maintain balance, harmony, respect, and received wisdom *across time and space*. Like the regenerative power of Torah in Jewish tradition (which teaches the community that the ultimate wisdom emerges from reciprocity, not authority), or the redemptive passion of the sacrificial atonement which occurs on the cross at Calvary for Christian communities, the salmon represent the infinite potential of the Great Mystery *to regenerate itself from itself.* Sacred compost. Infinite potentials of becoming. Furthermore, people are not only *witnesses* to this grand transformative dance; they are also an integral *part* of it. As humans living on this earth, we are, in fact, the ones being sacrificed, the ones being sacrificed to, and the ones offering the sacrifice. *Thou Art That.*

I wish to enter this discussion by first acknowledging the presence of these original caretakers of the land, their dignity, and their continued struggle for respect, restoration, and reparations. I honor their covenant with the land, and with their nonhuman

relatives, which, I believe, informed a set of cultural values that put them in direct contact with the great *mysterium tremendum* which is the source of all being and knowledge.

The world in which I am writing this is awash in strife, conflict, and branded, commercialized scripts that often highlight our differences from one another. There is deep political unrest in my country as election results are discredited, facts are contested as fictions, and the wisdom of the ancestors remains under constant assault from politicians, celebrities, professors, faith leaders, bankers, marketing firms, social media "influencers," and zealots of all stripes. Around the world, power brokers devise and implement the various mechanisms of coercion and control that seek to supplant the agency and identity of the Other, while solidifying and reinforcing status quo.

And yet, in some sense, this is the world in which humans have always lived. Traditionally mythologized stories of Us contain both the seeds of perpetual destruction and those of perpetual renewal. For untold generations, the sacred path has consisted of learning how to navigate these craggy, winding, and precarious spaces with dignity, compassion, and wisdom. If the stakes seem higher now, perhaps that is because now is the only reality we have. We exist only in the present, and must make our way to eternity through a thousand different versions of the right now: some glorious, others horrific, all transitory. Whatever right now "is," it is all we have. All we have ever had.

As chaotic and scary as the world feels, we have been here before. The world's wisdom traditions all emerged in just such times. Indeed, it is in the heart of the tempest that the map is most needed. It is in the belly of the beast that our cries for redemption are most authentic. It is during the generational, internecine battles to reestablish the Dharma that the compassion and timeless wisdom of the Lord is made manifest. In other words, it is *exactly* in times like these that we write and rewrite the mythic tropes that reveal the deepest aspects of our human potential. "Where you stumble, there lies your treasure,"[3] Joseph Campbell was fond of saying.

Joseph Campbell did more to popularize the study of myth and its relationship to human consciousness than any other figure of his time. Released shortly after Campbell's death on October 30, 1987, *Joseph Campbell and the Power of Myth* with Bill Moyers remains one of the most popular TV series in the history of public television, and continues to inspire new audiences to this day.[4] Campbell had a gift for making mythology come alive for people.

Cultures that derive from European descent have not become, as many philosophers in the last century predicted, post-religious or post-mythological societies. They have, however, experienced a series of collective and individual *mythic dissociations* that result in a rough sea of confusion, isolation, and increasingly desperate forms of self-destruction. But Campbell suggested these societies have not left mythological consciousness behind. Rather, he explored mythology to understand myth's role in shaping— and potentially *reshaping*—personal and communal identities. Campbell sought to discover who people *believe* themselves to be, in relationship to the mysterious Other. He investigated how different human communities gave shape to the invisible parts of themselves, and how these capacities could be called upon once again to help remake society and individuals according to what the emerging world required.

But what is myth, exactly? And what gives it this power to help make, and remake, the public and private constructions of the self?

Ernst Cassirer writes that myth is a "miracle of the spirit."[5] Myth doesn't necessarily refer back to an objective reality. It may refer to an internal, abstract, conceptual, or emotional reality. It is a language of symbols and metaphors. It can serve as a mirror and a guide to find the way *out of* and *deeper into* the self. It not only addresses deeper spiritual questions, but also validates the pursuit of them.

The poet Joan Walsh Anglund reminds us, "The bird doesn't sing because it has an answer. It sings because it has a song."[6] The "song" of mythology is *sung* to introduce the individual to the relational consciousness of the cosmos itself. A living myth helps its people learn to live and die well. It equips the individual, as Joan Didion once said, to leave this life as a satisfied party guest leaves a wonderful gathering at the end of the evening: full, whole, contented, and more intimately related to the other than before they arrived.[7] And with one overwhelming sentiment flowing from their spirit as they take their leave: gratitude. The following quote nicely summarizes our discussion so far: "If the only prayer you ever say is 'Thank you,' you have said enough."[8]

I was raised in a Mafia family that valued little more than whatever justified its own violent, criminal existence. Shotguns. Drugs. Laundered money. Sexual assault. These were the building blocks of my childhood. We moved every two years to another part of the country so my father could begin a new scam or avoid being prosecuted for a previous one. From New York to Southern California to Florida to Northern California.

Back to New York. Back to Florida. Arizona. From the center of everything to the middle of nowhere. We never put down roots. Running away from as much as we were running towards. Always running.

Growing up, I had to get used to being the new kid. Forced to define and redefine myself on a regular basis, I learned to get along with all kinds of people. White kids, Black kids, Asian kids, Latin kids. Christian kids, Jewish kids, Buddhist kids. From state and federal politicians to Hollywood actors and producers, from sanitation bosses in New Jersey to bikers in the High Desert of California, my childhood was a dangerous and fascinating sideshow of unique characters, unthinkable violence, rampant abuse, and general chaos. And even a bit of humor and wonder.

During this time, I developed a lasting fascination with the human story—that archaic narrative technology that binds us all together in our mutual quest for meaning and purpose. I also learned about many ways people distract themselves from awakening. But I found comfort in the arts and the quest for knowledge. Vonnegut, Bradbury, Hesse. Sagan, McKenna, Orwell. Huxley, Dali, Led Zeppelin. Kubrick, Scorsese, Lucas. Miles and Hendrix. Hurston and Angelou. Aretha. Peter Gabriel. Thich Nhat Hanh. Huston Smith. Joseph Campbell. Joanna Macy. Carriers of a wisdom I longed to know.

My home represented everything that has gone wrong with our species. It was a museum of decadence and violence. A shrine of generational shame and wasted opportunity. But these early artistic influences pointed me towards a greater reality that seemed both remote and immediate at the same time. The more I was introduced to the far-reaching contours of collective consciousness, the more I felt a sort of metaphysical homecoming. Like I was *remembering* a way of seeing that I had somehow already forgotten during my short life on earth. A way of perceiving the world that went beyond superficial appearances.

"To see, we must forget the name of the thing we are looking at," Monet once noted.[9] The modern world tried to trick me into settling for surface-level representations of the Other, but for my soul to survive I had to refuse to give in to those demands. For me, illumination is still as much a process of *forgetting* as it is of *learning* or *remembering*. I experience two kinds of forgetting: one that nourishes the soul, and one that devours it.

Hinduism has a similar concept with the notion of *moksha*, or liberation. The soul has become, according to this tradition, encumbered through successive lifetimes of bad thinking and behavior. It has forgotten who and what it truly is: the Absolute. So, through a program of rigorous self-transformation, or Yoga, the individual begins a process of *forgetting everything that made them forget* who they truly are. Eventually, the mythic dissociation is resolved and the individual is restored to a place of meaningful connection and purpose. They are liberated (*moksha*) from everything that separated them from the Absolute. To remember, they must first forget.

At an early age, I picked up a tattered and marked-up copy of Fritjof Capra's *The Tao of Physics* at a garage sale. I paid 25 cents for it. The right side of the book had been badly chewed by a family pet. I barely understood this bewildering text, often having to read a page, a paragraph, a sentence, over and over again. For some reason, I was driven to figure out what this book was saying: that the nature of the Cosmos revealed itself in a way that brought science and psychology together into a unified, quantum field of "nonlocal" consciousness.

I did not know what this meant. I only knew it was important. The book seemed to be suggesting that the world's wisdom traditions had, at their core, a shared understanding of the deep connection between consciousness and matter. And that emerging research from physics was confirming, not overturning, that shared mythological inheritance. One of the founders of modern theoretical physics, Max Planck, once noted, "I regard consciousness as fundamental. I regard matter as derivative from consciousness. We cannot get behind consciousness. Everything that we talk about, everything that we regard as existing, postulates consciousness."[10] In other words, in the Sanskrit language, *Tat Tvam Asi*: Thou Art That.

A few years later, I saw Bill Moyers interview Joseph Campbell on *The Power of Myth*. Everything changed again for me at that moment. I was 16 years old. Campbell had devoted his life to studying the metaphors, symbols, rituals, and narrative technologies that together told what he called "mankind's one great story."[11] Campbell did not, as some have suggested, diminish or dismiss the profound differences in the many ways humans have articulated the encounter with the sacred. Rather, he saw that complexity as an interconnected, diverse tapestry within which we could each find the ground of our own being. From the wreckage of my broken family, I discovered that my bliss was to immerse myself in this expansive world of big ideas and ancient truths. Campbell saved my life that day. I was looking for the home I had been denied by my family of origin. Mythology gave me something I had been denied through biology.

At his death in 1987, Campbell left a significant body of published and unpublished work that explored his lifelong passion. *"Tat Tvam Asi"* is a phrase that appears often in his collected spiritual reflections. Translated from the Sanskrit as *"Thou Art That,"* this compact incantation captures Campbell's generous spirit as well as his scholarly focus. These words, however, sparked much more than an intellectual curiosity for Campbell. Instead, the phrase stamped a "signature of celebration on his life and work."[12] He deeply understood the spiritual implications of the phrase across mythological traditions, and also strived to live by them.

The book *Thou Art That* is a compilation of previously unreleased essays and lectures by Campbell that focus on the religious metaphors of the Jewish and Christian traditions. Here Campbell explores mythological symbols, reexamining and reinterpreting them in the context of world mythology. Also included is editor Eugene Kennedy's interview with Campbell in *The New York Times Magazine*, which introduced Campbell and his work to the general public. Published in 2001, *Thou Art That* was the first title in the Joseph Campbell Foundation's series, *The Collected Works of Joseph Campbell*. Thus, the work occupies a special place in a publishing oeuvre that spans more than 70 years.

The central notion of the book—that we *are* or *contain* all that we seek—is primary to the exploration of Campbell's approach to mythology, symbol, ritual, and metaphor. For Campbell, the greatest mystical awareness occurs when the individual identifies with pure, generative consciousness, rather than with the vehicle of consciousness. The body is a vehicle of consciousness, but it is not the consciousness *itself*. Your thoughts are containers of individuated consciousness, but they are not *primary* consciousness itself. *Thou Art That. Tat Tvam Asi.*

In this view, we are not one with our bodies. We are not one with our brains and we are not a ghost in the machine. We are a greater, more expansive reality that expresses itself *through* a body and a brain. The body is just a window by which this greater reality is getting to know itself. Thou Art That.

The pages of *Thou Art That* contain a blueprint for how to read mythological traditions in a way that complements, rather than obscures, their vitality and common organizational principle: that the difference between the *inner* and *outer* worlds is an illusion that is shattered by a clear-eyed engagement with transcendence in all of its forms. Borrowing from psychologist James Hillman, the complexity of the human animal is animated, supported, and continuously reorganized by the awareness of being simultaneously "inside" and "outside" the alchemical containers used to study its own transformative processes.[13] In other words, we are simultaneously the *subject* and the *object* of spiritual discovery and mythic awareness, according to Campbell.[14] Mythology is the technology that allows us to occupy both positions at once. The key that unlocks these heavy, ornate doors of tradition, ritual, and sacrifice? Empathy.

Campbell drew this inspiration from Schopenhauer's question, "How is it possible that suffering that is neither my own nor of my concern should immediately affect me as though it were my own, and with such force that it moves me to action?"[15] This mysterious and somewhat illogical response to human suffering is rooted in empathy. From where does this impulse arise? Why does it seem to be the cultivated heart of most, if not all, of the world's wisdom traditions?

Schopenhauer's realization that "my own true inner being actually exists in every living creature. And is the ground of that comparison upon which all true, that is to say unselfish, virtue rests"[16] lies at the heart of Campbell's investigation of Jewish, Christian, and Hindu mythological systems. Empathy—the urge to respond to the suffering of the other as if it were our own—represents the breakthrough of a metaphysical response to suffering best rendered in the phrase "Thou Art That."[17]

We are embarking on an expedition to study the emotional and relational capacity of the human animal. This is not a purely academic exercise driven by intellectual abstraction and ideology. This is not a book that centers on the cultural, historical, and theological distinctions of the world's wisdom traditions. No, Campbell grasped that this primary spiritual realization was essential for understanding the metaphorical and symbolic language through which mythology and religion, whose images and narratives flow from a common source in the human imagination, ground and express themselves. Campbell saw the metaphors of mythology as emotional signs, derived through intuition and reflection on the play of the self through the forms of a local way of life. The goal of all true religion, according to Campbell, was to cultivate, in the individual and the community, an impulse toward ritualized, generative relations to the mystery of all existence: that of the self and the other.[18]

Through an expertly woven tapestry of the interplay between the ideas of Hinduism, Buddhism, Judaism, and Christianity, Campbell explores the metaphors of these religions and the overlap in their approaches to the soul on its journey back to itself. In this text, Campbell re-examines the primary functions of the symbol systems of Judaism and Christianity to uncover spiritual understanding and mystical revelation. In doing so, he exposes a fault line between those who accept religious metaphors to be historically true ("believers") and those who reject religious metaphors ("atheists"). The result, according to Campbell, is a society that largely misses the metaphorical and mystical grounding of its own symbolic heritage, leading to confusion, apathy, hostility, and mythic dissociation. Instead, we must look *beyond* the symbols, Campbell asserts, to the eternal, imaginative, and liminal space that constitutes the shared ground of our being and the cradle of all knowledge, wisdom, and forms.

And yet, the world's religions seem so different from one another. How can we compare the metaphysics of mythological systems that are, on the surface, so unique? Localized symbol systems can seem to exclude the possibility of comparison. The beliefs, rituals, and mythological narratives of others might seem irrelevant to our own lives and spiritual development. Judaism and Christianity in their own ways, for example, rest on the bedrock assumption of the oneness of God. Hinduism embraces over 330 million gods (and counting). How can these two systems be considered similar?

A partial answer can be found in two meanings of the word *human*. There are over 7.5 billion humans currently alive on this planet. Estimates of how many people have ever lived come in at around 107 billion.[19] Each of these individuals is a unique life force that has never entered the world before or after. Even twins are not wholly identical, and the reincarnated soul, if one believes in such a thing, is different from its previous forms. And yet, each is also fully and completely "human." Each is a small, but irreplaceable, aspect of that great caravan emerging from and heading toward a common mythic home. So the word *human* refers to one and many at the same time. No one is more or less human than anyone else. And we will never run out of new ways to express the concept of human. It is the same with divinity, which can be expressed with even less limitation than the concept of "human."

In the polyphonic chorus of mythological traditions, Joseph Campbell heard a shared sense of wonder, humility, gratitude, and awe at the mystery of being. Indeed it is in this perspective and its implications for the well-being of the relational self that I find the deepest and most lasting significance of myth.

I remember sitting in a seminary class on the book of Jonah. I was six years into a theological education at a conservative, evangelical Bible college. The professor, a kind but stern man who clung to a literal and historical interpretation of the text, had a diagram on the overhead projector of the inside of a whale's body. He pointed to a mucus-filled pouch inside the mouth and suggested a man could survive in this space for three days if the whale kept its mouth shut and the oxygen levels stayed constant.

Something in me died that day. I had devoted my life and education thus far to the study of the sacred, and had come to these stories and traditions with an open heart and a ravenous mind. I wanted to engage the wisdom of the ancestors. I had hoped to find, among outdated rituals, rules, and ceremonies, a lifeline to an ever-present transcendent reality. I wanted to know that One who cannot be known. To speak directly to the one referenced in the awe-inspiring prayer of Shankara, the Thomas Aquinas of Hinduism, that begins with the invocation, "Oh Thou, before whom all words recoil."[20] And I knew I would not get there by studying whale anatomy in an attempt to prove that the events within the biblical text actually happened. Existence itself was the only miracle I needed to set my curiosity ablaze.

I was not concerned with disproving the Bible either, mind you. No, I had other questions. What is it to know, in your deepest Self, the right thing to do and then find the motivation and courage to do it? What does it mean to run *from* instead of *towards* divine purpose because one is filled with fear, resentment, and anger, like Jonah? Jonah received a vision to deliver a message of love to a place called Nineveh: the capital of Assyria and the home of his tribal enemies. The power center who invaded Jonah's homeland and took ten of his twelve tribes into captivity, assimilation, and genocide. For a faithful Hebrew prophet, going to Babylon itself would be better.

What must the reluctant messenger have felt upon receiving this vision? Could God be just, if the mass murderers of his people were not brought to account by the same sword they used to annihilate all those they did not assimilate? "Yet forty days and Nineveh will be overturned." This was the prophet's message to the unrepentant people of Nineveh: forty days until divine justice would sweep through these halls of decadence and idolatry. But God also offers the possibility of forgiveness. A standard of justice rooted in mercy, not retaliation; in community, not tribe or empire. A reclamation of all space as Qadosh, as holy. Jonah conveys a covenant he doesn't fully understand.

A functioning mythology, according to Campbell, aligns individuals' consciousness to the mystery of the universe, helps societies engage with time and space, validates and supports the social order, and carries individuals through the stages of life. It is through this fluid, dynamic interpretive process that

Campbell evokes the living quality of biblical texts. To engage them as myths is not, as he asserts, to debunk them. Campbell's purpose in exploring myths is to reveal their living and nourishing core.

When Jacob wrestles with the angel of the Lord in Genesis 32, we must admit to ourselves, theists and atheists alike, that we have no idea whether or not this actually happened in the warp and weft of space-time. Either assertion is one of faith. But either way, the story's power resides in its mythic teachings. What is it to wrestle with the higher self? What is it to know who and what you are, to understand your place in the collective consciousness of your people, but struggle against this awareness because of fear, doubt, greed, pride, or ignorance? What is it to believe so strongly in your own conception of justice that you would challenge the deity over it? These are the mythological questions of the Jacob story that render the text relevant for modern readers.

Malidoma Somé speaks of an essence that dwells beyond the world of manifested forms. His Dagara people have no word for the "supernatural." They refer to this as "the thing that knowledge cannot eat." For Somé's culture, colonialist ways of knowing are limited by their binary cast. Everything is either sacred or profane, alive or dead, black or white, human or animal.[21] The enduring teachings of wisdom traditions speak of a reality beyond these limiting binaries, which is the source of their essential natures.

Thou Art That explores the Christian tradition in the context of the world's diverse yet unified mythos, exposing how an over-emphasis on historicity and exclusivity drain the stories and the religions of vitality, spiritual power, and relevancy as well as their cross-pollination with Hinduism, Buddhism, and the other wisdom traditions.

Thou Art That: A Skeleton Key Study Guide is for students, teachers, and other myth-minded readers. My intention is to summarize the content of Campbell's work, convey his creative and scholarly approach to myth, and illuminate interactive ways for you to expand upon and integrate his ideas with your own. The study guide includes chapter summaries, key themes, discussion questions, essay topics, suggestions for further study, and writing prompts. It is not a replacement for *Thou Art That*, but rather a guide and companion to help you dive more deeply and deliberately into the work of one of the most important mythologists of the modern era.

NOTES

1 Alan Watts, "The Nature of Consciousness," 1960.
2 *Chandogya Upanishad*, 6:2:1-2, 6:2:3a, 6:3:2, 6:8:7.
3 Joseph Campbell, *A Joseph Campbell Companion: Reflections on the Art of Living* (Joseph Campbell Foundation, 1991), "In the Field," Apple Books.
4 "Joseph Campbell and the Power of Myth," accessed August 31, 2023, https://billmoyers.com/series/joseph-campbell-and-the-power-of-myth-1988/
5 Ernst Cassirer, *Language and Myth* (Dover Publications, 1946), 14, 88-90.
6 Joan Walsh Anglund, *A Cup of Sun* (Harcourt, 1967), 15.
7 Joan Didion, *Slouching Towards Bethlehem* (Farrar, Straus, and Giroux, 2017), "Goodbye to All That," 225-238.
8 This quote is often attributed to the Christian mystic Meister Eckhart, but the first printed appearance is in a book called *A Bucket*

of Surprises (Lion Hudson, 2002) by J. John and Mark Stibbe.

9 Freeman Patterson, *Photography and the Art of Seeing* (Van Nostrand Reinhold, 1979), 10.

10 "Interviews with Great Scientists: VI—Max Planck," *The Observer*, January 25, 1931.

11 Joseph Campbell and Bill Moyers, *The Power of Myth* (Anchor, 1991), 64.

12 Joseph Campbell, *Thou Art That* (New World Library, 2001, xi.

13 James Hillman, *Alchemical Psychology,* Spring 2021, 256.

14 See Joseph Campbell, *Thou Art That*, "Appendix: A Discussion."

15 Campbell and Moyers, *The Power of Myth*, 110.

16 Ibid, 110.

17 Campbell, *Thou Art That*, xii.

18 Campbell and Moyers, *The Power of Myth*, 57.

19 Toshiko Kaneda and Carl Haub, "How Many People Have Ever Lived on Earth?" (Population Reference Bureau, November 15, 2022).

20 Huston Smith, *The World's Religions* (HarperOne, 2009), 60.

21 Malidoma Somé, *Of Water and Spirit: Ritual, Magic, and Initiation in the Life of an African Shaman* (TarcherPerigee, 1995), 15, 203-204.

Chapter 1
Metaphor and Religious Mystery

Chapter Summary

THE MEANING OF MYTH

Campbell begins this chapter with the story of an altercation he had with a radio host while promoting *The Historical Atlas of World Mythology*. Campbell encountered in the interview a very strong and narrow opinion of what a myth is, namely, a lie. But for Campbell, myth presents a version of the truth that is far more essential than the "facts" found in almanacs and encyclopedias.

In reply to the interviewer, Campbell defined myth as "an organization of symbolic images and narratives, metaphorical of the possibilities of human experience and the fulfillment of a given culture at a given time."[1] In other words, myth contains metaphors about our lives.

Definitions like this are what make Campbell such a *specialist* as a *generalist*. They are interdisciplinary, open, and yet still focused and mature in scope. Regarding the conversation with the radio host, Campbell observes:

> It made me reflect that half the people in the world think that the metaphors of their religious traditions, for example, are facts. And the other half contends that they are not facts at all. As a result we have people who consider themselves believers because they accept metaphors as facts, and we have others who classify themselves as atheists because they think religious metaphors are lies.[2]

Chapter I: Metaphor and Religious Mystery

Isn't it strange that we divide our vast compendium of collected knowledge into two fluid and ill-defined categories: *fiction* and *nonfiction*? On one side of the divide is that which we know we made up, but may contain truth: fiction. On the other side, that which we don't know if we made up, but may contain truth: nonfiction. This is an important admission about the slippery slope of being able to know anything at all with absolute certainty. We do not really know what is fully true about ourselves, our world, and our cosmos. Internally and externally, mystery abounds.

Mythic dissociation is an individual and social ailment that Campbell discusses frequently in this book. In contemporary cases of mythic dissociation, a limited understanding of their mythological symbols can hinder the vitality of entire cultures. Religious fundamentalism, scientific materialism, and consumerism all produce a loss of the creative, critical, and abstract thinking skills necessary to contextualize mythic symbols and rituals. But amazingly, these symbols and archetypes continue to emerge, regardless of whether participants understand their meaning. Surely, this is a sign that these things relate to a deep and enduring part of what makes us human.

WHAT MYTHS DO

Campbell next identifies four functions of myth that work together to guide individuals and cultures:

- **Metaphysical or mystical.** The first function of a living mythology is, according to Campbell, its metaphysical function—to awaken us to the mystery and wonder of creation, to an awareness of the mystical background of our lives. Because mystical insights are difficult to convey directly, myth speaks in metaphors, symbols, rituals, and symbolic narratives. This function, in Campbell's words, reconciles "consciousness to the preconditions of its own existence—that is, of aligning waking consciousness to the *mysterium tremendum* of this universe, *as it is*."[3] *Mysterium tremendum* is a Latin phrase Rudolf Otto uses in his book *The Idea of the Holy* to refer to the great, fearful, and awe-inspiring experience of the sacred.[4] Without the mystical component of myth, Campbell notes, we do not have a *mythology* but simply an *ideology*.

- **Cosmological.** Myth's cosmological function is to describe the physical universe so that the cosmos becomes vivid and alive, infused with meaning and significance. Every rock, hill, tree, flower, and star has its place and its meaning in the cosmological scheme the myth provides. In this unified image of the universe, all things are parts of a single, interrelated holy picture.

- **Sociological.** Campbell's sociological function of myth is that of establishing, validating, and maintaining a specific social order, authorizing its moral code as a construct beyond criticism or change. The sociological function is to pass down the law of the land (for example, Torah, Dharma, Tao, Marga): the moral and ethical codes for people of that culture to follow, and which help define that culture. The myth is made manifest in the behavior and relationships of the people.

"The gods themselves are simply agents of that great high mystery, the secret of which is found in mathematics. This can still be observed in our sciences, in which the mathematics of time and space are regarded as the veil through which the great mystery, the tremendum, shows itself."

—THOU ART THAT, *page 4*

- **Pedagogical or psychological.** This function addresses psychological challenges inherent in our biology that influence myths and rites. Through this function, myth can lead us through rites of passage that define the stages of our lives—from dependency to maturity to old age and, finally, to death, the final passage. These rites allow us to make the journey from one stage to another with a sense of comfort and purpose.

Therefore, a functioning mythology or religion will:

1) Help us to confront and make sense of our own mortality.

2) Help us know how to live in a confusing and volatile world.

3) Give us a sense of personal and communal identity.

4) Help us understand the cosmos and everything around us.

METAPHOR, THE NATIVE TONGUE OF MYTH

In this section, Campbell develops the idea that mythology is composed of metaphors: interlocking, dynamic, culturally informed metaphors that provide a roadmap to help the individual discover their purpose, plan, and place in the world. The rites, symbols, and sacred narratives of a given tradition are all aspects of one system.

Campbell connects mythic metaphors to Jung's "archetypes of the collective unconscious" and Bastian's "elementary and folk

ideas."⁵ One of Campbell's strengths is his ability to incorporate insights from other fields in order to reveal layers of meaning in many mythological traditions.

Campbell then speaks to the relationship between a living mythology and the artists of a given time and place. Artists use mythic metaphors in their work, which in turn shapes the myths. He observes that the metaphors and religious symbols of previous eras, especially when treated as historical facts, no longer captivate and energize minds and hearts as they once did. He predicts the emergence of new myths that arise from contemporary experience.

METAPHOR AND MYSTERY

Campbell connects the function of mythological metaphors with the experience of transcendent mystery. The goal of all religious metaphor, according to him, is to provide the individual and the community with a sense of participation in the divine field of meaning. The mystery encountered through mythic metaphors is not to be "solved" or concretely defined, as we would approach a mystery in the sciences. Rather, it is to be experienced directly, through the spiritual contemplation of symbols, which can offer a sense of the deep truths of human experience across all time and space.

Points of Interest

DO MOST PEOPLE MISUNDERSTAND?

The idea that "most" people misunderstand religious metaphor is an astonishing claim that is worth exploring in group discussions and writing prompts. Whether or not it is literally true,

Chapter I: Metaphor and Religious Mystery

it does provide some necessary context for the difficulties that arise when trying to discuss mythological themes and concepts with others. This is why Campbell's straightforward, modular, and expansive definitions work as great starting points for a collaborative journey of mutual discovery and connection to the great mystery that animates the cosmos.

THE NEED FOR A NEW MYTHOLOGY

In discussing the need for a new mythology, Campbell again demonstrates his lasting value to the study of human meaning-making. He does not rely on the old adage that traditional mythologies must be reformed or reinvigorated, but rather issues another claim: that the world is in a period of a mythological reshuffle. The old ways have become so detached from our lived experiences that Campbell suggests entirely new mythic systems will arise, organically, to assist us once again with some or all of his functions of myth.

MYSTERY IS TO BE EXPERIENCED

The notion of mystery as something to be experienced may seem strange in our world of scientific materialism, where mysteries are often seen as puzzles to be solved. To solve a mystery is to advance the cause of human knowledge, or to capitalize on new knowledge for the benefit of some business, social, or individual interest. To suggest that an unsolvable mystery rests at the center of existence itself and must be encountered and experienced directly without being fully understood is a radical claim that animates the imagination and very well might frustrate the ego.

"The life of a mythology springs from and depends on the metaphoric vigor of its symbols."

—THOU ART THAT, *page 6*

Chapter I: Metaphor and Religious Mystery

COMPLEMENTARY READING FROM CAMPBELL'S WORK

Campbell, Joseph. *The Inner Reaches of Outer Space: Metaphor as Myth and as Religion.* New World Library, 2012.

—. *The Mythic Image.* Princeton University Press, 1981.

—. *Myths to Live By.* Penguin, 1993.

—. *Pathways to Bliss: Mythology and Personal Transformation.* New World Library, 2004.

—. *Transformations of Myth Through Time.* Harper Perennial, 1990.

FURTHER READING

Armstrong, Karen. *A Short History of Myth.* Canongate U.S., 2006.

—. *The Great Transformation: The Beginning of Our Religious Traditions.* Anchor, 2007.

Barthes, Roland. *Mythologies.* Farrar, Straus and Giroux, 1972.

Harvey, Andrew. *The Essential Mystics.* HarperOne, 1997.

Malinowski, Bronislaw. *Magic, Science and Religion.* Lushena Books, 2022.

May, Rollo. *The Cry for Myth.* W.W. Norton & Company, 1991.

McGilchrist, Iain. *The Master and His Emissary: The Divided Brain & the Making of the Modern World.* Yale University Press, 2019.

Nietzsche, Friedrich. *The Birth of Tragedy from the Spirit of Music.* Penguin Classics, 1994.

Segal, Robert A. *Myth: A Very Short Introduction.* Oxford University Press, 2015.

Smith, Huston. *Why Religion Matters: The Fate of the Human Spirit in an Age of Disbelief.* HarperOne, 2006.

Discussion Questions

- How do you define *myth, mythology, metaphor, mystery,* and *mystical*? Where do your definitions come from?

- What is the difference between a metaphor and a lie?

- What is the difference between a religion and a mythology?

- What does it mean to explore a mystery that cannot be "solved"? Why might someone want to do so?

- Does focusing on the similarities between mythological traditions diminish the importance of their differences? If so, how? How might focusing on the differences between myths diminish the importance of their similarities?

- Do you agree with Campbell that "Half the people in the world think that the metaphors of their religious traditions, for example, are facts. And the other half contends that they are not facts at all"?[6] How does this align with your experiences of how religion and myth are discussed in your own family and community?

Essay Topics

- Campbell writes, "The gods themselves are simply agents of that great high mystery, the secret of which is found in mathematics. This can still be observed in our sciences, in which the mathematics of time and space are regarded as the veil through which the great mystery, the *tremendum*, shows itself."[7] Write an essay about what Campbell means by "the secret of which is found in mathematics."

- How does your mythological tradition align with Campbell's four functions of myth? Is there anything missing from Campbell's model that you consider an essential function of a living mythology?

- What modern artists are creating contemporary mythic metaphors? How are they doing this? What effect are these metaphors having on the community?

Creative Prompts

- Make a multi-modal project that contributes to the new myth. Write poems, do spoken word, write speculative fiction, make short films, paintings, or music that captures the symbols, traditions, and rituals of your emerging mythic forms.

- Using the four functions as a guide, create a photo essay showing how you fulfill each in your own life.

"Metaphors only seem to describe the outer world of time and place. Their real universe is the spiritual realm of the inner life. The Kingdom of God is within you."

—THOU ART THAT, *page 7*

- Mystery, "Oh, Thou before whom all words recoil."[8] Use a medium other than language to communicate something about your experience or understanding of transcendence.

- Write a poetic piece that compares insights gleaned from Campbell's work with that of a spiritual teacher, such as the Buddhist monk Thich Nhat Hahn:

    This body is not me.
    I am not limited by this body.
    I am life without boundaries.
    I have never been born,
    and I have never died.[9]

NOTES

1 Joseph Campbell, *Thou Art That*, 1-2.
2 Ibid, 2.
3 Ibid, 2.
4 Rudolf Otto, *The Idea of the Holy*, 1936.
5 Campbell, *Thou Art That*, 6.
6 Ibid, 2.
7 Ibid, 4.
8 Huston Smith, *The World's Religions* (HarperOne, 2009), 60.
9 Thich Nhat Hanh, *Chanting and Recitations from Plum Village* (Parallax Press, 2000), 188.

"*There can be no real progress in understanding how myths function until we understand and allow metaphoric symbols to address, in their own unmodified way, the inner levels of our consciousness.*"

—THOU ART THAT, *page 8*

Chapter II
The Experience of Religious Mystery

Chapter Summary

In this chapter, Campbell unpacks how religious mystery is experienced in various traditions and mythic systems we have created to cultivate and chaperone the divine relationship to self.

SYMBOLISM AND RELIGIOUS EXPERIENCE

Traditions that see God as separate from the world include Christianity, Judaism, Islam, and Zoroastrianism. In these religious systems, an important goal is to establish a relationship with the divine being.

Campbell emphasizes that in this view, humanity lives in a fallen world. Divinity, or God, exists outside of the individual, who can only build a relationship with God through a religious institution or church. This split, or dissociation, between people and God Campbell calls *mythic dissociation*.

What's more, these religious institutions often treat scripture stories as history and scientific fact. When contemporary history and science contradict scriptures, people can feel a sense of alienation from their religion. Campbell extends this idea to propose that the gap between a person's lived experience and their religion's image of God can actually invalidate the person's sense of feeling like themselves and living a full life.

"*The first aim of the mystical is to validate the person's individual human experience.*"

—THOU ART THAT, *page 12*

Chapter II: The Experience of Religious Mystery

EXPERIENCING MYSTERY

The alternative to mythic dissociation and alienation is the experience of mystery, or a feeling of awe so profound and so far beyond day-to-day experience that is often described as religious, or sacred. Functioning myths can bring about this experience, which Campbell considers the religious, or mystical, function of mythology.

This experience can involve a realization that the individual is not separate from divinity at all. In other words, a person's deepest essence is ultimately the same as the essence of the entire cosmos. Religious traditions in Asia emphasize this unity of the individual and the all.

Campbell theorizes that these religious experiences might be unusual for people trained in religions, because religion tends to rely on names and labels that get in the way of experiencing that which is beyond names and labels. Further, these experiences are completely unique to each individual.

Campbell identifies two approaches to meditation on the path to experiencing mystery. The first is called *discursive meditation,* and involves holding a religious scene in the mind's eye. *Ordered meditation,* on the other hand, goes far beyond this mental exercise to an experience that transcends images and ideas. Discursive meditation can act as a way station on the way to and from experiences of ordered meditation.

Campbell demonstrates these modes of meditation with a few meditative paragraphs about the symbolic connections between Christianity and earlier traditions, such as Egyptian deities like

Osiris and Set, and the Greek figure of Orpheus. Campbell speculates that St. Paul himself recognized these parallels, as well as parallels between the story of the Garden of Eden and the crucifixion. The tree in Eden ushered in pairs of opposites like good and evil, while the "tree" of the cross points the way back to unity. "*These* are the mysteries,"[1] Campbell writes, meaning the experience of oneness beyond daily life and discursive meditation.

Similar representations of duality appear on ancient ceramics, such as a vase that shows Triptolemus, Hermes, and wheat on one side, and on the other, Dionysus, a satyr, and wine.

Campbell points out a duality in approaches to religion: One approach focuses on ethics and the duality of good and evil; the other more mystical perspective focuses on going beyond all dualities, including the duality of good and evil. The first of these pits followers against nature, and the second aligns followers with nature.

Campbell sees in the three Graces an image similar to the Christian Trinity, except represented as female figures. The Father corresponds to the Grace Thalia, or abundance. The Son is Euphrosyne, or rapture. The Holy Spirit is Aglaia, or splendor. But ultimately, in Campbell's view, the gender of the image doesn't matter, because the experience of transcendence goes beyond those labels.

Points of Interest

THE BEAUTY OF IDEAS AND WRITING

Notice how Campbell's prose flows from one symbol system to the next. The way he moves from the Christian mythic symbols to the Hindu and back again models a way of seeing both that makes

each more accessible, more alive, more complex and, strangely, more unique. Notice also Campbell's short chapters, the accessibility of the work, and how much is packed into these few pages. Consider following this example and trying to communicate the essence—the distilled wisdom and energy—and essential truths of your experience in concise, engaging language.

ENTERING THE DEPTHS OF WISDOM

The work reveals wisdom from the spiritual knowledge of our ancestors. Like Huston Smith said of the *Tao Te Ching*, this work can be read in a half an hour or in an entire lifetime.[2] Give careful thought to the ideas Campbell explores in these pages. Open inquiry, humility, wonder, awe, and a deep appreciation for the sacredness of the Other should be the basis for exploring these inner and outer spiritual landscapes.

BRUSHING UP AGAINST THE MYSTERY

The essence of this book is found in this chapter, in many ways. The Kingdom of Heaven is with you. Tat Tvam Asi. Thou Art That. And That is ultimately a Mystery. We are, as Carl Sagan once said, the Cosmos becoming aware of itself.[3] So this means, as the wisdom traditions have always taught us, that each of us is a unique manifestation of the whole.

THE THERAPEUTIC COMPONENT

Often victims of trauma, especially childhood trauma, are left with a lingering question of "Why?" We search for the "cause" of which the *effect* was the trauma we experienced, as if to bring a sense of justice or closure to the wound by solving this mystery.

"Faith, we might say, in old-fashioned scripture or faith in the latest science belong equally at this time to those alone who as yet have no idea of how mysterious, really, is the mystery of themselves."

—THOU ART THAT, *page 13*

"Who, then, may speak to you, or to any of us, of the being or non-being of God, unless by implication to point beyond his words and himself and all he knows, or can tell, toward the transcendent, the experience of mystery."

—THOU ART THAT, *page 13*

Campbell's approach to mystery, however, reverses the script and turns mystery into the *source* of healing, restoration, and freedom for the wounded individual. We are not defined by what happened to us but by a deeper, grander, more unified mystery. Campbell is aligning us with the mystic awareness of being itself.

ECOLOGY AND TRANSFORMATION

In his ethnographic research with the Oglala Sioux medicine man Black Elk, Joseph Epes Brown noted:

> *We are still very far from being aware of the dimensions and ramifications of our ethnocentric illusions. Nevertheless, by the very nature of things we are now forced to undergo a process of intense self-examination; to engage in a serious re-evaluation of the premises and orientations of our society. The inescapable reality of the ecological crisis, for example, has shattered for many a kind of dream world, and has forced us not only to seek immediate solutions to the kinds of problems which a highly-developed technology has fostered, but also, and above all, to look to our basic values concerning life and the nature and destiny of man.*[4]

Black Elk represented a way of seeing, of relating, to all the living that constitutes an indigeneity of wildness: an experiential encounter with the Other that renders both transparent to transcendence, as Joseph Campbell would put it, and centers the regenerative mystery of nature. A reclamation of this way of relating to the external world begins with a radical transformation of the self. The implications of this for deep and generative models of ecological restoration, community support, and educational reform are worth exploring.

Chapter II: The Experience of Religious Mystery

Complementary Reading from Campbell's Work

Campbell, Joseph. *The Hero with a Thousand Faces*. New World Library, 2008.

—. *Myths to Live By*. Penguin, 1993.

—. *Pathways to Bliss: Mythology and Personal Transformation*. New World Library, 2004.

—. *Romance of the Grail*. New World Library, 2015.

Further Reading

Herschel, Abraham. *The Prophets*. Harper Perennial Modern Classics, 2001.

Swami Adiswarananda. *The Four Yogas: A Guide to the Spiritual Paths of Action, Devotion, Meditation and Knowledge*. SkyLight Paths, 2007.

Huxley, Aldous. *The Perennial Philosophy*. Harper Perennial Modern Classics, 2009.

"When one is ready to see the eternal flashing, as it were, through the latticework of time, one can experience mystery."

—THOU ART THAT, *page 15*

Chapter II: *The Experience of Religious Mystery*

Discussion Questions

- Campbell states about Christian mythology, "Here also is the revelation that one life can be personified as a Deity, as in the Christian tradition, and everything comes from the Deity. But the personification is not what is important. What we have is a trans-theological, transpersonified revelation."[5] What might he mean by this, and how does it align with more orthodox interpretations of the Christ narrative? What is gained, and lost, by adopting Campbell's approach to the myth?

- Campbell makes a distinction between the mythological systems of the "East" and the "West," comparing and contrasting how each approaches concepts such as mystery, sin, divine essence, and mystical awareness. Does this distinction still hold? What about the mystical schools of Judaism, Christianity, and Islam, as well as the Indigenous traditions of the Americas? What about aspects of Hinduism and Buddhism and Confucianism that emphasize obedience over identification?

- "Faith, we might say, in old-fashioned scripture or faith in the latest science belong equally at this time to those alone who as yet have no idea how mysterious, really, is the mystery of themselves."[6] What might Campbell mean by this statement? How can mystery stand in opposition to faith?

Essay Topics

- Campbell states in this chapter "the first century question, whether Christianity was a mystery religion or *the* mystery religion of which all the others were re-figurements, is relevant. The many symbols, such as the animals of the Egyptian mystery religions breathing their spirit on the infant Jesus—the bull of the god Osiris and the ass of his brother Set, there in the manger—suggest their early understanding that this was indeed so. So, too, in the same nativity scene, the Magi wear the hat of Mithra as they pay homage."[7] Write an essay exploring the parallels between two mythological stories. What should we make of parallels in symbolism, theme, and motif? How does the overlap affect our understandings of each narrative?

- Campbell compares the essential natures of the three Greek Graces with the functions of the Christian trinity. He likens the role of Euphrosyne, rapture, to that of God the Son who sends forth the divine radiance into the world. He compares Aglaia, splendor, to the Holy Spirit, who brings us back to the presence of the divine. And he likens God the Father to Thalia, abundance, who unites the two in an eternal, co-creative embrace. Write an essay about how these connections do and do not work.

Chapter II: The Experience of Religious Mystery

- Campbell offers the story of the apostle Paul's mystical experience on the road to Damascus as an example of how discursive meditation can be used to gain greater insight into the mystery of being. Write an essay exploring another historical, fictional, or mythological example of this transformative experience. Examples include the Buddha's enlightenment, the moment a family member immigrated to another country, and the experiences of characters in fiction. Use your imagination and explore this theme for all its richness and deep connectivity between place and inner landscapes.

CREATIVE PROMPTS

- Campbell likens the symbolism on an ancient Roman vase to the elements of the Roman Catholic Mass. Write a story, poem, screenplay, or other piece that explores another work of art or culture that bridges two cultures and resonates with the themes from each.

- Experiment with artistic works that explore the experience of divinity existing within yourself, and divinity existing somewhere outside yourself.

- J.B.S. Haldane in an essay titled "Possible Worlds" states, "Now, my own suspicion is that the universe is not only queerer than we suppose, but queerer than we *can suppose*" (emphasis added).[8] Meditate on what this means to you. Create a piece of art, writing, or music that reflects on this idea.

NOTES

1 Joseph Campbell, *Thou Art That*, 15.
2 Huston Smith, *Tao Te Ching: Mystical Classics of the World: The Classic Book of Integrity and Way* (Bantam Doubleday Dell Publishing Group, 1998), "Introduction."
3 Carl Sagan, *Cosmos: A Personal Voyage: The Shores of the Cosmic Ocean*, Episode 1, 1990.
4 Joseph Epes Brown, *The Sacred Pipe: Black Elk's Account of the Seven Rites of the Oglala Sioux* (University of Oklahoma Press, 1953), xv.
5 Campbell, *Thou Art That*, 15.
6 Ibid, 13.
7 Ibid, 14.
8 J.B.S. Haldane, *Possible Worlds and Other Papers* (Harper & Brothers, 1928), 298-99.

"The experience of mystery comes not from expecting it but through yielding all your programs, because your programs are based on fear and desire. Drop them and radiance comes."

—THOU ART THAT, *page 16*

Chapter III
Our Notions of God

Chapter Summary

This chapter begins with an exploration of our experience of reality as described by the philosopher Immanuel Kant. Kant points out that time and space form the backdrop for everything we experience. Space and time separate us from each other and from what we experience.

This leads Campbell to pose the question, "Is there a God?"[1] God, Campbell says, cannot exist only within space and time. The word points to a reality beyond the things, or "facts," that we experience. He suggests the techniques of Zen to address the problem: always referencing something with an equally weighted pronouncement of its absence. Whatever is must also not be.

How do we, in other words, conceptualize that which lies beyond all constructed forms of knowledge? And how can we relate to that which is not defined by the limitations of its own being? How do we understand that which is not bound by space or time when we experience everything through these two ever-present filters?

The answer is through religious metaphor and symbol, meaning that which provides us, according to Campbell, with "metaphorical references, connotations, this side of that ultimate reach, opening the mystery of the operation of this transcendent energy in the field of space and time."[2] But we must never forget that the menu is not the food itself. It is, as another well-known

"Is there a God? If the word 'God' means anything, it must mean nothing. God is not a fact. A fact is an object in the field of time and space, an image in the dream field. God is no dream, God is no fact—'God' is a word referring us past anything that can be conceived or named."

—THOU ART THAT, *page 17*

metaphor reminds us, a "finger pointing at the moon." Is the god a source, Campbell asks us, "or is the god a human manner of conceiving of the force and energy that supports the world?"[3]

God can be imagined as a "final term,"[4] meaning God is the ultimate reality. Gods can also be imagined as personifications of various intermediaries between the world and that ultimate, unknowable sacred reality. They can become "transparent to transcendence,"[5] as Campbell says, and so should we. We should identify with the consciousness that shines through us rather than the bodies through which our consciousness shines. In this shift lies the realization of "Thou Art That,"[6] or your essential nature is divine.

Campbell illustrates this point with the image of light shining through light bulbs. When a bulb burns out, light cannot shine through it anymore. To identify with the body is like identifying with the bulb; to identify with consciousness is like identifying with the light.[7]

Similarly, the Arthurian image of the Waste Land corresponds to a way of living that is cut off from the realization of our own divinity. Restoring the Waste Land requires authentic alignment with our own essential nature.

Effective myths provide spiritual and psychological support in times of difficulty. They connect us with the sacred dimension beyond space and time.

ELEMENTS OF OUR EXPERIENCE OF THE MYSTERY OF GOD

Campbell revisits the mystical and psychological functions of a working mythology and how each contributes to emotional states of mystery, awe, and gratitude. Psychologically, mythic images of external places can be interpreted to mean inner landscapes, and myths about the future are referring to possibilities in the present.

Biblical stories that scholars trace back to earlier Sumerian and Babylonian myths replace mother images with father images—a father without a wife. These images make no sense to the psyche, Campbell suggests, and served more to establish the dominance of a patriarchal system than to open to transcendence.

This transcendence is the essential nature of all things. One way to approach it is first to identify not as an object, but as the witness of your body and experience, and then to let go even of being the witness.

In Abrahamic religions, mystics have been tortured for suggesting similar ideas. When humans are seen as entirely separate from God, there can be no divinity within a person. Instead, people are to have a relationship with God. These traditions tend to interpret symbols as references to historical facts in the field of space and time.

SYMBOLS: OUT OF TIME AND PLACE

Religious symbols do not refer primarily to history, according to Campbell. Their reach and power is universal and comes from within.

Campbell challenges the authority of dogma over experience. We should be wary, he writes, of any dogma that tries to tell us how to respond to the symbols of a mythological tradition.

Tradition is important, and the connection to the ancestors runs through a shared experience of the symbol, but it is activated by an authentic encounter with the transcendent Other in the here and now. It can never be fully contained, and thus fully defined. "The individual's assent to a definition is not nearly as important as his or her having a spiritual experience by virtue of the influence of the symbol."[8]

Campbell asserts that one of the unique capacities of the human animal is the ability to experience awe in the presence of the mystery of being. We may challenge whether or not this is true based on a more developed understanding of animal psychology than we had access to when Campbell was alive, but the question remains: What is the role of mystery, awe, and wonder in the creation of the identities we weave of ourselves and others inside of the mythic constructs we inhabit? Campbell equates the "birth" of the ability to experience awe with the image of the Virgin Birth.

Campbell wants us to consider how reading the symbols of mythological narratives can "shed the dross of history for the immediacy of our experience of mystery."[9] We exchange certitude for curiosity, wonder, and awe. We exchange dogma for mystery. And we exchange a relationship of obedience for one of identification.

The emergence of the individual as the center of moral, social, and psychological import in the modern world drastically differs from the social and mythological constructs of the past. In the past, we had the Torah, the Tao, the Dharma, the Marga to lead us all into the presence of righteousness and transformation. But we no longer get there through simple obedience and

"In almost all other systems, the gods are agents, manifestations, or imagined functionaries of an energy that transcends all conceptualization. They are not the source of the energy but are rather agents of it."

—THOU ART THAT, *page 18*

faith to what came before. "One must search out one's own values and assume responsibility for one's own order of action and not simply follow orders handed down from some period past,"[10] Campbell notes in this section. Even if we do engage with one of the mythological traditions of previous generations, we must do so with fresh eyes, each of us responsible "in his or her own way, to themselves and to their world."[11]

We can no longer rest in the rigid, comfortable binary of us versus them. "We can no longer speak of 'outsiders,'"[12] Campbell asserts. "We have now to learn somehow to quench our hate and disdain through the operation of an actual love, not a mere verbalization, but an actual *experience* of compassionate love, and with that fructify, simultaneously, both our neighbor's life and our own."[13]

Campbell finishes the section, and the chapter, with a discussion of what he calls the "romantic quality of the West."[14] This yearning for the uniqueness of individual experience sits at the heart of the Western ethos, according to Campbell. But is it enough? We find ourselves today leaning back towards the need for community, for connection, for the deep and abiding web of identity that emerges from us, from we, instead of I and me. How to reconcile the two? How to walk a path of individual experience, dignity, and awe while tracing the steps of one's ancestors, even as one becomes an ancestor to those that come after? How to walk when we know each step draws us closer to end of the world? The Kingdom made manifest in the flickering lights of our persistent, imaginative, integrative, and wondrous awe? Knowing each path is determined as much by its end as it is by its beginning?

Chapter III: Our Notions of God

Points of Interest

ASSOCIATING CONSCIOUSNESS WITH THE METAPHOR OF LIGHT

I love the way Campbell begins this chapter by highlighting the limits of our perception—that which exists within the field of space and time—then moves the discussion to the example of lights in a room as a metaphor for embodied consciousness. This metaphor illustrates so much and is readily accessible for almost any age group and level of education.

THE CONTINUAL RETURN TO AWE

Campbell always brings us back to mystery, symbol, and metaphor. This keeps us humble, curious, and filled with awe, even as it draws us ever closer to the flame of illumination that we seek to understand in ourselves and in the larger cosmos.

MYTH AND PSYCHOLOGY

"You can take this precept as a basic theological formula: a deity is the personification of a spiritual power, and deities who are not recognized become demonic and are really dangerous. One has been out of communication with them: their messages have not been heard, or, if heard, not heeded. And when they do break through, in the end, there is literally hell to pay."[15] Here, Campbell nicely articulates the basic premise of psychological healing modalities that are emerging in recent years such as eye movement desensitization and reprocessing (EMDR) and Internal Family Systems (IFS). Campbell hints at this integrative approach again in this chapter when he writes, "The goal in psychiatry, it is said, is to bring the mental structure that

is governing our lives into accord with this energy that comes from forces we do not fully understand and cannot locate."[16] For more on this, see the work of Dick Schwartz in *No Bad Parts: Healing Trauma and Restoring Wholeness with the Internal Family Systems Model* (Sounds True, 2021).

Complementary Reading from Campbell's Work

Campbell, Joseph. *The Inner Reaches of Outer Space: Metaphor as Myth and as Religion.* New World Library, 2012.

—. *Oriental Mythology; The Masks of God, Vol. 2.* New World Library, 2021.

—. *Occidental Mythology: The Masks of God, Vol. 3.* New World Library, 2022.

—. *Romance of the Grail: The Magic and Mystery of Arthurian Myth.* New World Library, 2015.

Further Reading

Abelard, Peter and Héloïse. *The Letters of Abelard and Héloïse.* Penguin, 2004.

Eckhart, Meister. *The Essential Sermons, Commentaries, Treatises and Defense.* Paulist Press, 1981.

Eliot, T.S. *The Wasteland and Other Poems.* Vintage, 2021.

Goodall, Jane. *My Friends, the Wild Chimpanzees.* National Geographic Society, 1967.

Kant, Immanuel. *Critique of Pure Reason.* Cambridge University Press, 1999.

Pagels, Elaine. *The Gnostic Gospels.* Vintage, 1989.

"This may be somewhat hard to grasp. But when the god closes himself and says, 'I am God,' he closes you, too, because this says you are just a fact and so the relationship in these terms is between you and the fact that is no fact."

—THOU ART THAT, *page 18*

Watts, Alan. *Behold the Spirit: A Study in the Necessity of Mystical Religion*. Vintage, 1972.

—. *Beyond Theology: The Art of Godmanship*. New World Library, 2022.

—. *This Is It: and Other Essays on Zen and Spiritual Experience*. Vintage, 1973.

—. *The Two Hands of God: The Myths of Polarity*. New World Library, 2020.

—. *The Way of Zen*. Vintage, 1999.

White, T.H. *The Once and Future King*. Berkley Medallion, 2021.

Discussion Questions

- What do you think Campbell means when he says we should become "transparent to transcendence"?

- In this chapter, Campbell states that in Judaism and Christianity, "God is a final term."[17] What might he mean by this? Do you agree with this assessment? Are there any notable exceptions in Judaism and Christianity? What about Kaballah and Christian Mysticism? Is God a "final term" for these interpretive approaches as well?

- Campbell suggests in this chapter, "In this modern world of ours, in which all things, all institutions, seem to be going rapidly to pieces, there is no meaning in the group, where all meaning was once found. The group today is but a matrix for the production of individuals. All meaning is found in the individual, and in each one this meaning is considered unique."[18] Do you think this is still true today? Has the proliferation of the internet changed this? Is this sentiment true across all cultures and people groups?

Essay Topics

- Compare and contrast the language of Jesus with that of the prominent teachers of Hinduism, Buddhism, Taoism, and other systems of Eastern thought. Where are they similar? Where are they different? What does this teach us about each system and the links Campbell draws between them? Do we do a disservice to any of the traditions by highlighting the ways in which they are similar to one another?

- While discussing "The Wasteland" as a space of wounded, broken people leading inauthentic lives, separated from their own hearts, Campbell states, "You can take this precept as a basic theological formula: a deity is the personification of a spiritual power, and deities who are not recognized become demonic and are really dangerous."[19] What "deities" have become dangerous by not being recognized as spiritual powers?

"*We should become transparent to transcendence."*

—THOU ART THAT, *page 18*

- Campbell suggests that to appreciate the language of religion, which is metaphorical, "one must constantly distinguish the denotation, or concrete fact, from the connotation, or transcendent message."[20] He then goes on to give of an example of how this method works by examining the connotation of the biblical notion of the "End of the World." What other religious symbols can we examine through this lens? What do we learn about symbols like the Trinity, Hell, Angels and Demons, the Virgin Birth, and other religious metaphors once we examine them for their transcendent, hidden meanings?

Creative Prompts

- "Ultimately, man should not ask what the meaning of his life is, but rather must recognize that it is he who is asked."[21] Given what Campbell develops in this chapter about the nature of self and its deep connection to the Source of all that exists, what is the meaning of life? Explore possibilities here through a number of mediums, including poetry, music, art, dance, and prose.

- Write a dramatic dialogue between parts of your personality. How would you imagine a conversation would go between your personal self and the universal, expansive, unbound consciousness that Campbell suggests is the source of your deepest "identity"?

NOTES

1 Joseph Campbell, *Thou Art That*, 17.
2 Ibid, 18.
3 Ibid, 18.
4 Ibid, 18.
5 Ibid, 18.
6 Ibid, 20.
7 To better explain this, on page 21 Campbell points to two simple terms used by the Japanese to refer to these conditions. One refers to "the realm of the world of the individual," and the other to "the world of the general." The Japanese have a saying that roughly translates "Individual, general, no obstruction." They follow this with a variation that reads "Individual, individual, no obstruction." No obstruction, according to Campbell, means they are substantively the same.
8 Campbell, *Thou Art That*, 29.
9 Ibid, 29.
10 Ibid, 30.
11 Ibid, 30.
12 Ibid, 30.
13 Ibid, 30.
14 Ibid, 31.
15 Ibid, 23.
16 Ibid, 18.
17 Ibid, 18.
18 Ibid, 31.
19 Ibid, 23.
20 Ibid, 19.
21 Victor E. Frankl, *Man's Search for Meaning* (Beacon, 2006), 113.

"The fundamental, simple, and great mystical realization is that by which you identify yourself with consciousness, rather than with the vehicle of consciousness. Your body is a vehicle of consciousness."

—THOU ART THAT, *page 20*

Chapter IV
The Religious Imagination and the Rules of Traditional Theology

Chapter Summary

The role of religion, Campbell says, is to "awaken the heart"[1] by interpreting religious symbols in spiritual ways. Interpretations that focus on ethics and politics fail to provide an experience of the mystery of being. When clergy people misinterpret religious metaphors in this way, artists can perform this work.

Campbell references Aristotle and James Joyce to define the "tragic emotions" of *pity* and *terror*.[2] Pity here refers to the feeling that arises when witnessing the kind of suffering we all share in. Terror, on the other hand, is an encounter with suffering and its "secret cause," which elicits a feeling so sublime that it goes beyond pain.[3]

These tragic emotions, pity and terror, hold the potential to break us past the appearance of any phenomenon, usually presented through pairs of opposites in the fields of space and time, and directly to a rapture. This rapture unites us with human suffering, the human sufferer, and the "secret cause."[4]

The secret cause of our lives is the Source. The secret cause of our deaths is our destiny. In this frame, death is a homecoming, a return, a fulfillment of all that we came into this life to accomplish. As an example, Campbell cites the assassination of Dr. Martin Luther King Jr., who lived into his destiny and his death through his courageous leadership toward justice.

This way of living requires saying *Yes* to life and to destiny. In Campbell's view, saying *Yes* allows our lives to "open up to radiance."[5] This is the metaphysical experience that religious symbols are meant to create. For example, the metaphor of the Promised Land can be interpreted as an aspect of your inner world, not as a geographical location on a map.

IMAGINATION AND ITS RELATION TO THEOLOGICAL INQUIRY

Campbell introduces this section by citing a sixteenth-century painting in the Vatican that shows the Egyptian goddess Isis seated on a throne and teaching two students: Moses and Hermes. This image illustrates the Renaissance combination of two views about the sacred. Moses represents the view that the divine is transcendent, meaning very far away, and Hermes represents the "hermetic" tradition which sees the sacred in all things.[6] This dual view is central to the relationship between imagination and theology.

Campbell describes what C.G. Jung termed the "active imagination" as a means for individuals to fathom their own creative depths. Since mythic images emerge from deep parts of the psyche, active imagination allows the individual to encounter them in ways that allow the images to "speak back" to those same intimate spaces and psychic depths.

Campbell connects mysticism and active imagination to a passage in Corinthians II where Paul discusses visions that can't be described. These concern the transcendent aspect of divinity that exists beyond all thoughts and ideas. Campbell finds it helpful to compare how different traditions point to this indescribable experience. He considers them all to be "mutually illuminating."[7]

"When the clergy do not or cannot awaken the heart, that tells us that they are unable to interpret the symbols through which they are supposed to enlighten and spiritually nourish their people."

—THOU ART THAT, *page 33*

Biblical traditions, on the other hand, view the deity as a local god associated with their particular people. This makes it more difficult to connect with religions other than one's own, and it has served to suppress goddess traditions in particular. Campbell sees the emerging symbolism of Mariolatry as a return of this impulse.

Points of Interest

THE BETRAYAL OF THE CLERGY

Campbell makes a bold claim at the beginning of this chapter that clergy are betraying the human race if they fail to awaken hearts and instead spend their time and energy talking of ethics and political problems. He is not upset that clergy are conservative. He is not upset that clergy are liberal. He is not upset that the clergy, as individual humans, have political values, beliefs, and affiliations. He *is* upset, however, at clergy who have traded in their ability to conjure wonder, awe, and life-affirming gratitude towards the mystery of existence for a megaphone through which to assume "heavy involvement in regulating the intimate decisions of family life."[8] These observations are even more relevant today than when Campbell wrote them.

MYTH, IMAGINATION, AND ART

Campbell uses terms like *imagination* and *art* in precise and expansive ways. These terms are fundamental to his understanding of the aesthetic scope of living mythologies, the social and psychological complexity of human beings, and the cultural forms they create. Most fascinating to me is the sense that to Campbell, terms like *art* and *imagination* are as much verbs—sacred, holy actions—as they are products or objects for analysis.

"There lies the key to art. It is beyond the pairs of opposites, beyond desire or fear. This transformation is the experience of the sublime."

—THOU ART THAT, *page 36*

Chapter IV: The Religious Imagination and the Rules of Traditional Theology

THE GODDESS RE-EMERGING

In this chapter, Campbell is vocal about his views of the suppression of goddess traditions by "ruthlessly patriarchal" systems.[9] He calls out the cognitive dissonance this suppression induces through religious images that make no sense, such as a man (Adam) giving birth to a woman (Eve).[10] He seems to hope that the Women's Movement might have a positive role to play on this topic, and he sees Mariology as a form of resurrection of the sacred feminine in a Catholic context.

COMPLEMENTARY READING FROM CAMPBELL'S WORK

Campbell, Joseph. *Man and Myth* (audiobook). Joseph Campbell Foundation, 2002.

—. *Mythos* (video series). Acorn Media, 2012.

—. *Primitive Mythology: The Masks of God, Vol 1*. New World Library, 2020.

FURTHER READING

Gurevich, Andrew. "Artistic Origins." Joseph Campbell Foundation MythBlast series January 21, 2021.

Hannah, Barbara. *Encounters With the Soul: Active Imagination as Developed by Carl Jung*. Sigo, 1981.

Joyce, James. *A Portrait of the Artist as a Young Man*. Penguin Classics, 2003.

Von Franz, Marie-Louise. *Alchemical Active Imagination*. Shambhala, 1997.

Marlan, Stanton, and David Rosen. *The Black Sun: The Alchemy and Art of Darkness.* Texas A&M University Press, 2005.

Merton, Thomas. *Zen and the Birds of Appetite.* New Directions, 1968.

Porete, Marguerite. *The Mirror of Simple Souls.* Paulist Press, 1993.

Spearing, A.C. *The Cloud of Unknowing (and Other Works).* Penguin, 2001.

Strand, Sophie. *The Madonna Secret.* Bear & Company, 2023.

Discussion Questions

- Campbell says at the very outset of this chapter that the "problem for and function of religion in this age is to awaken the heart."[11] What do you think he means by this? Do you agree or disagree? Why?

- Campbell claims that every theological tradition must set up a set of "game rules"[12] if it wishes to translate and convert mystical experiences into the dominant theological tradition of the day. Do you agree or disagree? Why?

Chapter IV: The Religious Imagination and the Rules of Traditional Theology

- In the Editor's Foreword to *Thou Art That*, Eugene Kennedy writes that Campbell has been taken to task for saying the reformed Roman Catholic Mass reduces the celebrant to a role similar to Julia Child's.[13] This is the chapter where he makes that reference.[14] Discuss Campbell's reasoning and comment on whether you think critics have accurately characterized his comments.

- Campbell states that the "Promised Land" is not any one, single location but is "a corner of the heart, or any environment that has been mythologically spiritualized."[15] Do you agree or disagree? How does it compare to other concepts of "Holy Land" or "Promised Land"? What are the social and legal implications of seeing the concept this way?

Essay Topics

- Select an artist who you believe "awakens the heart" through their work. Write an essay summarizing their background, their work, and how their art speaks to the theological importance of art and the imagination.

- Research the differences between Moses and Hermes. How would they each interpret a few specific biblical symbols, metaphors, or passages? Explore the differences and similarities between how you imagine them interpreting each one.

"All religions are ethical in their foreground. But there exists a metaphysical ground beyond good and evil, beyond I and Thou, beyond life and death. When the symbol is opened, that background is what shines through and forth."

—THOU ART THAT, page 36

- How has Mariolatry reintroduced the tradition of goddess veneration? How is it similar to and different from the cults of Inanna, Isis, Ishtar, and Aphrodite in Rome around the time of the origins of the Christian tradition?

Creative Prompts

- Explore the concept of the "active imagination" by meditating on a religious symbol from a tradition outside of your own. After a period of calming the mind, ponder the symbol and notice how it makes you feel. Research the symbol and find out as much as you can about it. How is it encountered in the tradition from which it arose? Where do your meditative reflections align with and diverge from that?

- Create a piece of art in any medium that "awakens the heart."

- Make a map of the world as you inhabit it and sanctify it.

Chapter IV: The Religious Imagination and the Rules of Traditional Theology

NOTES

1 Joseph Campbell, *Thou Art That*, 33.
2 Ibid, 34.
3 Ibid, 34.
4 Ibid, 34.
5 Ibid, 36.
6 Ibid, 37.
7 Ibid, 40.
8 Ibid, 33.
9 Ibid, 42.
10 Ibid, 42.
11 Ibid, 33.
12 Ibid, 37.
13 Ibid, xix.
14 Ibid, 33.
15 Ibid, 36.

"The Promised Land is not a place to be conquered by armies and solidified by displacing other people. The Promised Land is a corner of the heart, or it is any environment that has been mythologically spiritualized."

—THOU ART THAT, *page 36*

Chapter V
Symbols of the Judeo-Christian Tradition

Chapter Summary

In this chapter, Campbell unpacks specific Biblical symbols to show how they reveal themselves differently depending on whether we emphasize their literal (*denotative*) or their metaphorical (*connotative*) meanings. He moves effortlessly from the rituals, symbols, and metaphors of Judaism and Christianity to their corollaries in Zoroastrianism, Hinduism, Platonism, and the work of Freud and Jung. Campbell weaves these strands together to reveal sacred truths that are as relevant today as when they were first uttered and written.

WHAT KIND OF GODS HAVE WE?

Campbell begins with a discussion of the biblical Flood narrative as a way to discuss two mythologies it contains. One is that of the planting cultures of ancient city states, for whom the idea of a flood was a cyclical event. The other is that of nomadic desert people, whose myth is of a more personal God who creates the world and people who are meant to obey him.

These are entirely different conceptions of God, according to Campbell. The first offers deity as a metaphor for the dynamism of life. The other is a God who is "out there"[1] and fashions the cosmos as separate from himself. A God that is a fact. One who is closed, separate, and unflinchingly authoritative.

Campbell connects cyclical, agricultural myths with mathematically cyclical aspects of the natural world. For example, the number 432 recurs in the cycle of the zodiac and the beat of the human heart. This number also appears in Hindu, Icelandic, and Babylonian myths, as well as the passage of years in the book of Genesis. Campbell offers this connection as a "hint," he says,[2] that Genesis contains both mythological conceptions of God.

The mathematical movements of the cosmos gave rise to the idea of the universe as "a living being in the image of a great mother"[3] whose womb contains us all. This allows us to imagine ourselves as microcosms of the macrocosm, which helps us live in harmony with nature.

Mythological rejections of the natural world arose around two thousand years BCE, particularly in Jainism and Zoroastrianism, which pit righteousness against evil and nature. This view makes sense in cultures for whom the natural world presented more threats than sustenance, such as desert nomads.

Campbell highlights two definitions of the word *transcendent*. The term can mean very far away, as is the case with Yahweh, and it can also mean "the ultimate mystery of being that transcends all conceptualization, beyond thought, beyond categories."[4] The divine is transcendent in this second sense in the Hindu Upanishads and in Gnosticism, which emphasizes the experiential realization of the sacred that is best described through metaphor.

Religious symbols are misunderstood when interpreted as historical facts. They open up to transcendence when interpreted as metaphors.

GENESIS

In this section, Campbell guides us through the liminal landscape of Eden to explore its mythical and metaphorical dimensions. He insists that the Eden story reveals its deepest layers of meaning through a psychological reading of the narrative.

Genesis contains two creation stories, according to Campbell, which contain elements of both kinds of mythological systems.

When Adam and Eve eat the fruit, they learn about pairs of opposites such as good and evil, male and female. God exiles them from the garden. In order to return, they would have to set aside the impulse to judge. They would have to move past the pairs of opposites, which the story shows as the pair of cherubim guarding the gate. Campbell finds a similar message in the metaphors of Buddhism, Jesus, and Gnosticism.

In the second myth in Genesis, Adam names the animals and God creates Eve out of Adam's rib. Campbell connects this to other myths of the original androgyne from Hinduism, Plato, and the Kabbala: the separating and coming back together of the divine creative impulse, which Campbell mentions in the previous section.

ABRAHAM, FATHER OF THE JEWISH PEOPLE

Campbell summarizes Genesis 12, in which the couple Abram and Sarai become Abraham and Sarah to mark the "transformation of consciousness"[5] in which they become the spiritual parents of a people.

"All of our religious ideas are metaphorical of a mystery."

—THOU ART THAT, *page 48*

The Akkadian emperor Sargon has a similar birth story to Moses. Each of them was released into a river as an infant inside a basket made of rushes. Each was found and raised by a royal household. These stories with no supernatural elements Campbell calls legends, or "vaguely remembered history into which symbolic themes have been grafted."[6] Stories with deities as characters he calls "pure mythology."[7] The history is not the important part; the mythological metaphors are.

The sacred stories and symbols of the Hebrew people bind them together as a people. "Who went down, we ask. The Patriarchs went down. What came out? A people."[8] In the tradition of Judaism, Campbell continues, the people are the sacred thing.

Campbell references Thomas Mann's novel *Joseph and His Brothers*, which tells of Jacob and Esau and contains parallels to the Egyptian brothers Osiris and Set. Characters like Joseph live according to the "mythological imperative"[9] to follow a calling to lead their people. These stories, as in the case of Moses, often begin with an infant cast off by the birth family and raised by another family.

Eventually Moses leads the people out of Egypt, but the date of this event is not important. What's important is that the story forges them into a holy people.

The Bible shifts out of myth and into history with the books of Chronicles and Kings. Later stories also include some legends as well as history.

"The central myth of the Bible is that of exile," Campbell observes.[10] In his view, the Christian tradition tells of a return to the garden. Jesus gives up pairs of opposites by claiming his oneness with God. These stories are often interpreted historically rather than spiritually and metaphorically. They can still have great spiritual effect, however, as in the tradition of Judaism, which "offers a realization of a divine principle working in a holy people."[11]

Campbell shares that he grew up in the Catholic Church. He left that church because he was unable to reconcile the myth as fact, as it had been presented to him. Only after studying mythology did he realize that the mythic power of the biblical narratives provided bridges and opportunities for reconciliation of his rational and spiritual selves. It was with great joy that towards the end of his life he was able to find a path back to an appreciation of the Church and its teachings as experienced through a mythological and metaphorical set of cognitive lenses.

The chapter closes with Campbell's advice to read the Bible "spiritually rather than historically. Read the Bible in your own way, and take the message because it says something special to each reader."[12] Just don't assume that your way of understanding God is anyone else's way.

Points of Interest

GOD AS FACT VS. GOD AS METAPHOR

This idea is, perhaps, the backbone of this book and Campbell's entire approach to mythology. He reminds us that we cannot identify with God when we think of God as a fact. God is a symbol. The meaning of the symbol lies beyond all naming, beyond all categories of thought. However, when we think of

Chapter V: Symbols of the Judeo-Christian Tradition

God as a metaphor for the dynamism of life, and attach ourselves to that, we are God. In this space, we enter into direct communion with the ground of our very being.

THE MATHEMATICS OF MYTHOLOGICAL SYMBOLS

Campbell offers a brief discussion of a topic that is often misunderstood, or ignored, by scholars of religions and mythology. He begins with the observation that the old mythologies recognized a vital connection between the human heartbeat and the "pulse" of the cosmological order. This "as above, so below" construction formed the basis of the old cosmologies and is present in the structure of the religious traditions that followed. It is a truth that remains with us today, and gives our experience of the physical universe with a vibrant beauty.

OVERCOMING FEAR AND DESIRE AS THE PATH BACK TO THE GARDEN

This section seems to grow more relevant with time. The modern individual is beset with triggers that keep their fear inflamed and their desires ravenous. But here Campbell roams, in his characteristic way, through the world's wisdom traditions to ground our awareness of how these archaic systems can help us overcome fear and desire. "What, then, is the way back into the Garden? One must overcome the fear and the desire."[13]

THE DENOTATIVE VS. CONNOTATIVE POWER OF MYTHOLOGICAL SYMBOLS

To free ourselves from the limitations of the strictly denotative, or literal, renderings of our mythological symbols is to revitalize them, to liberate them and ourselves, from the cage they have

"That is what the story of the expulsion from the Garden of Eden is all about. It is not about an historical incident but about a psychological, spiritual experience, a metaphor for what is happening to us right now."

—THOU ART THAT, *page 51*

been stuck in for too long. To embrace their connotative, or metaphorical, meanings is to see how our myths nourish, sustain, and connect us to each other and to the ground of our being. "All of our religious ideas are metaphorical of a mystery. It is vital to recall that if you mistake the denotation of metaphor for its connotation, you completely lose the message that is contained in the symbol."[14]

Complementary Reading from Campbell's Work

Campbell, Joseph. *The Masks of God, Vol. 4: Creative Mythology.* Penguin, 1991.

—. *The Mythic Dimension: Selected Essays 1959–1987.* New World Library, 2017.

—. *Goddesses: Mysteries of the Feminine Divine.* New World Library, 2013.

—. *The Mythic Image.* Princeton University Press, 1981.

—. *Joseph Campbell Audio Collection Vol. 1: Mythology and the Individual.* HighBridge Company, 2002.

—. *The Inner Reaches of Outer Space: Metaphor as Myth and as Religion.* New World Library, 2002.

Further Reading

Blake, William. *The Marriage of Heaven and Hell.* Dover Publications, 1994.

Hamilton, Heather. *Returning to Eden: A Field Guide for the Spiritual Journey.* Quoir, 2023.

Kant, Immanuel. *The Critique of Pure Reason.* St. Martin's Press, 1965.

Mann, Thomas. *Joseph and His Brothers: The Stories of Jacob, Young Joseph, Joseph in Egypt, Joseph the Provider.* Everyman's Library, 2005.

May, Rollo. *Freedom and Destiny.* W.W. Norton & Company, 1999.

Merton, Thomas. *Zen and the Birds of Appetite.* New Directions, 1968.

Pagels, Elaine. The Gnostic Gospels. Vintage, 1989.

Rank, Otto. *The Myth of the Birth of the Hero: A Psychological Interpretation of Mythology.* Martino Fine Books, 2011.

Zimmer, Henrich. *Philosophies of India.* Princeton University Press, 2020.

Discussion Questions

- What do you think Campbell means when he says that mythological symbols have become "so familiar that they have become static and brittle"[15]? Do you agree or disagree? Can you think of any examples that support his assertion? Can you think of any that challenge it?

- Campbell suggests that "two mythologies are found in the story of the flood."[16] Summarize these two mythologies and comment on how each is present within the Flood narrative. How does this awareness change our reading of the story?

- Discuss the anecdote at the end of the chapter regarding his interaction with Martin Buber. What do you think of the encounter? Is Campbell being insensitive or dismissive of the cultural and theological traditions of Buber? Is he displaying an understanding of the connections among the world's mythological systems? Perhaps both?

- Campbell cites Jesus's statement that says, "I and the Father are One."[17] Discuss this insight in light of the observations Campbell makes in this chapter about the twin mythological constructs of relationship and identification with the Divine.

Essay Topics

- Do a comparative analysis of the biblical flood story with that of another mythological tradition (for example Babylonian, Sumerian, or Vedic). What deeper understandings of the metaphor are revealed by comparing and contrasting the similarities and differences between the different approaches to the story of a great flood?

- Develop a cross-cultural, interdisciplinary analysis of the theology and symbolism of exile across a number of distinct mythological traditions.

"These mythic themes can be regarded as just fairy tales, or they can become illuminations for your life. And all of this symbolism is in the Genesis text when it is read in terms of its connotation—that is, the true metaphorical meaning that gives us its spiritual message and significance."

—THOU ART THAT, *page 53*

- Research the Greek Eleusinian mysteries and explore how they are, as Campbell puts it, a coming together of the two different mythologies he discusses in this chapter. How do they exemplify the overcoming of fear and desire that keep one out of the metaphorical Garden, and also a return to the nature-centered religious impulse to bring oneself into accord with the cycles of nature?

Creative Prompts

- Select a mythological symbol from a tradition you are not familiar with and write a short essay detailing what feelings, thoughts, and emotions you experience while contemplating the image. How does it communicate its connotative, or metaphorical, meaning to you? If you wish, after this direct spiritual encounter with the symbol, look up its full context and denotative meaning and compare what you find with your initial response to it.

- Create a poem, a song, a sculpture, a piece of art, that uses principles of mathematics to communicate some symbolic and metaphorical truth.

- Look around the world as though looking at the Garden of Eden. Record what you "see" in a poem, a piece of art, a song, or a short story.

- Write a narrative essay that tells your family's origin story and how it creates a mythos that holds the family together in common identity, purpose, and community. If you like, feel free to write a different origin story for you or your family, making the story what you would like it to be.

Chapter V: Symbols of the Judeo-Christian Tradition

NOTES

1 Joseph Campbell, *Thou Art That*, 44.
2 Ibid, 45.
3 Ibid, 45.
4 Ibid, 47.
5 Ibid, 53.
6 Ibid, 54.
7 Ibid, 54.
8 Ibid, 55.
9 Ibid, 56.
10 Ibid, 57.
11 Ibid, 58.
12 Ibid, 60.
13 Ibid, 51.
14 Ibid, 48.
15 Ibid, 43.
16 Ibid, 43.
17 Ibid, 57-58.

"Water always represents the realm below the field of manifestation, the place of new energy, the new dynamism. It refers to the field of the unconscious, going down into that realm and coming back out of it."

—THOU ART THAT, *page 55*

Chapter VI
Understanding the Symbols of Judeo-Christian Spirituality

Chapter Summary

Campbell begins this chapter by making a distinction between religions of creed, or belief, and those of birth, or ethnicity. He sees Christianity, Buddhism, and Islam as religions of creed, or belief. Buddhism began with the life the Buddha in the sixth and fifth centuries BCE. Christianity began with the life of Christ around the turn of the Common Era, and Islam began around the time of the Hejira, or the journey of the prophet Muhammad and his people from Medina to Mecca, in 622 BCE.[1] The "ethnic religions,"[2] according to Campbell, are those which one is born into, such as Hinduism, Judaism, and Shinto.

The rest of the chapter is devoted to a deep dive into motifs of the Christian symbol system and how they can initiate psychological transformations that support the religion's enduring power.

THE VIRGIN BIRTH

Campbell weaves threads from James Joyce, Hindu and Buddhist traditions, Navajo, Celtic, and Christian myths to explore the motif of the Virgin Birth. In this common image, a mythic child's father is absent or unknown, and the child often matures into a spiritual leader. Read as a metaphor rather than a biological fact, this symbol encourages us to ask who or what functions as our spiritual father.

Chapter VI: Understanding the Symbols of Judeo-Christian Spirituality

To illustrate this motif, Campbell tells the Hindu story of the virgin birth of the saint Vyasa. The section concludes with a reminder that the denotation, or literal interpretation, of this motif "leads to argument rather than awe."[3] The connotation, or spiritual interpretation, "accents its religious significance."[4]

THE CAVE

Here Campbell addresses the mythic motif of a divine birth in a cave. This symbol has associations with the winter solstice, or the longest night of the year. The ancient Persian and Roman god Mithra, "the Lord of Light,"[5] was born at this time, which is why December 25 was chosen to celebrate Christmas.

Caves often serve as the setting for initiation rituals, where initiates experience "the birth of the light"[6] in their own hearts and souls, which Campbell also connects with the moment when light first appears in creation myths.

He finishes this section with a fascinating exploration of early depictions of the Christian nativity scene. One of these shows the Magi wearing hats connected to Mithra, and the animals are the ass and the ox, which were associated with the Egyptians gods Set and Osiris, respectively. So the image shows earlier deities gathered to honor a new god.

THE INFANT

Stories of the spiritual infant often include themes such as no room at the inn and the infant in exile, which suggests the metaphorical idea that "the new world is born outside the province of the old."[7]

The Massacre of the Innocents is another aspect of the infant motif, one which shows the resistance of the ego and the powers-that-be to the rise of new ideas. Recalling the Hindu story of the birth of Krishna, Campbell shows how the tyrant tries to kill any potential threats to his kingship. Ultimately the fresh ideas of the new, youthful king are exactly what will unseat the tyrant.

FLIGHT INTO EGYPT

In Jesus's flight to Egypt, Campbell sees a variant on the story of the Israelites leaving Egypt. Both spend forty days in the desert. Campbell believes that Christianity was originally intended as a change within Judaism, and only began extending to Gentiles with the apostle Paul.

THE CHILD AS TEACHER

The amazing deeds of mythic children illustrate what powers the child will grow into. For example, the child Heracles kills snakes. The young Christ teaches the wise men in the temple. The young Buddha's body held signs that the child would become either a king or a teacher. Later in their tales, Buddha and Jesus both study with the greatest teachers they can find, and then go beyond them.

Campbell ends the section with a discussion of the political and sociological waves of Hellenization and revolt that rocked the Mediterranean world at the time the young Jesus was coming of age. The tumult seemed to fulfill the prophecies of "the end of the world"[8] which led to apocalyptic religious movements.

"The biography of a mythological savior is itself an image statement of the sense of the doctrine. It becomes attached to the personality of the savior-hero in a way that legends become attached to all great figures."

—THOU ART THAT, *page 62*

THE MESSIAH

In the Persian tradition of Zoroastrianism, a Messiah would appear at the end of the world, just before a final battle. In the Hebrew tradition, the Messiah would be a more political figure: a king who would create a nation for Israel. The Essenes were a Hebrew sect who combined these two ideas, notably in the teachings of John the Baptist.

Campbell sees the ritual of baptism as a metaphorical second birth. The waters of baptism suggest the image of the fish, which remains important in Christianity. For some ancient Christian groups, Jesus's baptism marks the moment he became the Savior. In this view, he was born human, not divine, which avoids the implication that Mary was a goddess.

Both Jesus and Buddha, after studying with the best teachers available, retreat to the wilderness for a time of solitude. Both are tempted by devilish adversaries who offer worldly delights, and both resist the temptations. Both then return to the world to teach their own insights. Campbell connects these stories to the Orphic image of the world as a metaphorical ocean that imperfectly reflects the lights of the sky. Spiritual teachers point the way out of the murky waters and into the immediate experience of that other reality.

MIRACLES

Miracles such as walking on water and healing the sick are common in religious traditions, including Christianity. But this does not necessarily mean that they didn't happen. Seemingly miraculous cures have been documented, and spiritual treatments

may be effective for psychological difficulties, but these stories offer metaphorical meanings as well. For example, the miracle of the loaves and fishes connects to the many repetitions of the mythological image of the fish in the Christian tradition.

THE LAST SUPPER

Campbell points out Easter and Passover occur around the same time as the Greek observance of the death and resurrection of Adonis in springtime. The Greek and Christian traditions both focus on an individual figure dying and rising again, while the Jewish tradition celebrates the metaphorical resurrection of an entire people. Moses guides the people, but he is not the focal point of the story.

JUDAS

Biblical and Jain legends include an antagonist, or "counterplayer"[9] to the hero, and eventually the two characters reconcile.

Campbell sees Judas differently, however. Campbell suggests that Jesus didn't predict Judas's betrayal; instead, Jesus assigned Judas this role in the drama because Judas was spiritually developed enough to understand what needed to happen. Judas is, according to Campbell, the "midwife of salvation, the counterplayer to Christ."[10] He functions quite consciously as Christ's shadow.

In contrast, Jesus assigns Peter the more organizational role of leading the church because Peter is not as spiritual as Judas. In Buddhism, the figure of Ananda has a similar role to Peter.

Chapter VI: Understanding the Symbols of Judeo-Christian Spirituality

CRUCIFIXION

"Why did Christ have to die?"[11] In this section, Campbell summarizes the two main answers to that question during medieval times.

One answer was that this tricked the devil. God gave his son to the devil in place of mankind, but Christ's divinity prevented the devil from keeping him.

The other answer was to atone for Adam and Eve's sin, which was so awful that only God himself could make up for it, by dying in the form of a man.

THE CROSS

Interpreted literally, the image of the cross refers to the historical event of Christ's Crucifixion, which redeemed humanity from the effects of the events in the Garden of the Eden.

A Guatemalan shrine at Palenque called the Temple of the Cross also honors a divine savior named Kukulcan in the Mayan tradition and Quetzalcoatl in the Aztec. This figure, whose name means Feathered Serpent, also had a virgin mother, died and was reborn, and will return again in the future. The Christian and Mayan crosses have both been depicted with a bird on top, and a death mask or skull at the base.

For all these reasons, Campbell asserts that the significance of the cross is mythological, not historical. Campbell further connects the image of the cross to the world tree Yggdrasil in the Icelandic *Edda*. The god Othin hung on that tree for nine days and nights in order to acquire divine wisdom.

"People with a certain value and impact of character act very much as magnets for the mythic materials that float always in the air. As they become attached to these figures, they form themselves into constellations around them, illuminating their character and their teaching."

—THOU ART THAT, *page 62*

Chapter VI: Understanding the Symbols of Judeo-Christian Spirituality

Yggdrasil and the Cross both depict the metaphorical center of the universe, like mandalas. C.G. Jung situates his four psychological functions around the compass points of a mandala, which are where the arms of a cross point as well. Jesus on the cross, then, becomes an image of wholeness, connecting and transcending all pairs of opposites: up and down, left and right, heaven and earth, life and death. The image invites us to forego the imbalance of the pairs of opposites in favor of taking up residence in the center, where we open up to "a circulation of energy and light through all four of the functions."[12]

In the Christian cross, the horizontal beam rests above the center of the vertical beam, at the location of the heart. Christ, then, represents the spiritual possibility of transcending pairs of opposites through the heart.

THE END OF THE WORLD

Churches have tended to see the end of the world as an event that has yet come to pass. But this drains the symbol of its mythological power. Mythologically speaking, the "end of the world" is not an event in time but a radical shift in perception. In this shift, the individual becomes able to see and affirm "the world's radiant joy" or "the dynamism of life in all things."[13]

Points of Interest

WHO WENT INTO EGYPT? WHO CAME OUT OF EGYPT?

Campbell observes that it was the Patriarchs who went down to Egypt, but it was the people, the community, who came out. The metaphor of going into the watery abyss as an individual

but returning as a member of a living community is profound here. A bridge between the previous age and the coming one, a bridge for traversing the subconscious. And Moses is not the hero; the people, animated by this new covenantal relationship to their deity, are the hero. But in the Greek and Christian traditions, it is not that one is of a race, it is rather that one is an individual who has achieved a certain transformation of the psyche through a form of confession and belief. This latter is a *psychological* transformation, placing the clear emphasis on the experience of the individual. The sense of these motifs is similar, however: the emergence of the new thing from "the land of mud." Egypt was considered the land of mud, the land of the flesh. From it wisdom comes as well as pain, and the Jews emerged from Egypt as the Savior emerges from the tomb. So Passover, Easter, and the resurrection of Adonis are all symbolic of the birth of something new out of the earlier darkness. That place of deep, dark mystery from which we all emerge and to which we all return.

JUDAS AS THE COUNTERPART TO THE SAVIOR

Campbell has such a wonderful take on the role of Judas in the Passion narrative. We are so quick to vilify, so in need of a scapegoat that we may miss the subtle brilliance of this character. Judas is the "midwife of salvation,"[14] Campbell asserts in this chapter. His role is a sacred one. There is no salvation without him. There is no light without the shadow. What a wonderful meditation on our own shadows. What a wonderful opportunity to reflect on the things we have had to let go of in ourselves for the new self to be born.

THE END OF THE WORLD

The end of the world happens every day. Warfare, disease, death, and suffering all lead to the loss of self and all that one holds dear. But Campbell is referring to another kind of "end," one that transcends but includes all notions of loss, grief, and disillusion. An end of the world that emerges from a radical shift in perspective. An end to the illusion that one is separate from the cosmos. You die to the egoic self and take up the full sense of your own identity in relationship to the transcendence that is in you and in everyone and everything else.

Complementary Reading from Campbell's Work

Campbell, Joseph. "The Interpretation of Symbolic Forms." *The Binding of Proteus: Perspectives on Myth and the Literary Process.* Associated University Press, 1980.

—. *Occidental Mythology: The Masks of God, Vol. 3.* New World Library, 2022.

Further Reading

Armstrong, Karen. *A History of God: The 4,000-Year Quest of Judaism, Christianity and Islam.* Ballantine Books, 1994.

—. *A Short History of Myth* (Canongate U.S.; First Trade Paper edition; October 1, 2006)

Patton, Laurie L. (trans). *The Bhagavad Gita.* Penguin Classics, 2008.

"Who comes out of the water? And, who went into the water? Who went into the water were the patriarchs. Who came out, were the people. And Moses is not the hero; the people, the Jewish people, are the hero."

—THOU ART THAT, *page 74*

Eliade, Mircea. *The Myth of the Eternal Return: Cosmos & History*. Princeton University Press, 2018.

Girard, Rene. *Things Hidden Since the Foundation of the World*. Stanford University Press, 1987.

May, Rollo. *The Cry for Myth*. W.W. Norton & Company, 1991.

Crawford, Jackson. *The Poetic Edda: Stories of the Norse Gods and Heroes*. Hackett, 2015.

Rohr, Richard. *The Universal Christ: How a Forgotten Reality Can Change Everything We See, Hope For, and Believe*. Convergent Books, 2021.

Spong, John Shelby. *Liberating the Gospels: Reading the Bible with Jewish Eyes: Freeing Jesus from 2,000 Years of Misunderstanding*. Harper San Francisco, 1996.

Discussion Questions

- What are the differences between religions of creed and religions of birth? Can you think of any traditions that skirt the line between the two?

- Campbell suggests that when we focus on the denotative, or historical, referents of mythological symbols like the Virgin Birth or the Resurrection, we sacrifice their deeper, connotative power and thus create "argument instead of awe."[15] Do you agree with this assessment? Why or why not?

"The Kingdom is here, right before our eyes— that is the message of Jesus in the Gospels."

—THOU ART THAT, *page 83*

Chapter VI: Understanding the Symbols of Judeo-Christian Spirituality

- In this chapter, Campbell claims that the first depiction of the crucifixion of Jesus that we have comes from a boys' school in Rome and was likely created for the purposes of bullying one of the children there. What are the metaphorical, psychological, and sociological implications of this: that the earliest representation of one of the greatest religious symbols of the modern world emerged from an incident where a child was being bullied by his peers?

Essay Topics

- Compare and contrast the similarities and differences between the Christian Apocalypse/Savior narrative and that of Zoroastrianism.

- Campbell mentions in the chapter that the ox is the sacred animal associated with the Egyptian god Osiris and the ass (donkey) is the sacred animal of the Egyptian god Set. But he does not mention how these associations came to be. Write an essay exploring how these deities came to be associated with these particular animals and what the connotative and perhaps denotative reasons were for these early associations.

- Write an essay exploring the metaphorical implications of the sacrifice of Othin, the crucified Feathered Serpent Quetzalcoatl, or the death of Osiris, and situate your findings within the culture the symbol emerges from. In other words, what are the symbolic and mythological layers of significance of these symbols to the cultures from which they emerged?

CREATIVE PROMPTS

- Which section of this chapter did you find the most interesting or surprising? Create a piece of art, writing, music, or dance about the imagery in that section.
- Create a piece of art, a poem, a short story, a song that represents how "the end of the world" has manifested in your life as a psychological transformation of death to the old and birth of the new. This can be descriptive or aspirational.

NOTES

1 Joseph Campbell, *Thou Art That*, 61.
2 Ibid, 61.
3 Ibid, 65.
4 Ibid, 65.
5 Ibid, 65.
6 Ibid, 65.
7 Ibid, 67.
8 Ibid, 69.
9 Ibid, 75.
10 Ibid, 75.
11 Ibid, 76.
12 Ibid, 82.
13 Ibid, 83.
14 Ibid, 75.
15 Ibid, 65.

"You see the world's radiant joy and you say 'Yes' to it all and you do not say 'No' to it at all."

—THOU ART THAT, *page 83*

Chapter VII
Question Period

Chapter Summary

This chapter contains a selection of audience questions from the live lectures collected in this book, as well as Campbell's answers.

Q: "Can you explain what you mean by the 'problem' of mythology in our time?"[1]

Campbell sees three main issues with contemporary mythology. First, myths are dismissed as factually false, which drains away their psychology energy. Second, religions insist mythic symbols are historically true, which science proves to be nonsense. This also drains the emotional energy out of the images. Third, Freud collapsed the meaning of myth into one interpretation of one particular family dynamic. It now falls to the individual to reinvigorate mythological symbols by combing through the wreckage of these broken systems to find the images that activate our imaginations and connect us to the sacred ground of being from which these symbols and systems emerge.

Q: "Does the mythic motif of the 'Hero's Journey' apply to the Judeo-Christian tradition?"[2]

Campbell offers two examples of figures from biblical traditions whose stories follow the mythological cycle of someone who leaves their people, passes a test of some kind, and returns with a benefit for the people. Moses goes up the mountain and returns with the Ten Commandments. Christ goes to the desert, passes

"A mythological image is one that evokes and directs psychological energy. It is an energy-evoking and energy-directing sign."

—THOU ART THAT, *page 86*

the test of the devil, and returns to redeem people from the system of laws. He preaches a new message of the spirit, a message of love animating the law instead of the other way around.

Q: *"Does this apply to us? Are we 'heroes' on a spiritual journey?"*[3]

Campbell answers this question by placing side by side the images of the Holy Grail and the Catholic Mass in medieval Europe. The Mass offered a generalized experience of the sacred, but the Grail quest tested the character of each individual. This is not an either-or moment; Campbell simply offers both images of encountering the sacred. Similarly, he sees a contemporary need to educate young people by helping them to develop their own unique character, "without overdoing it."[4] This is ultimately a spiritual quest.

Q: *"Rebirth seems a recurring theme. Can you explain more about its symbolism?"*[5]

Campbell offers two primary images of rebirth. The first is the moon, which appears to die and be reborn, symbolizing the "miracle of rebirth"[6] here in the field of space and time. The serpent is also a part of this mythic symbolism, because as it sheds its own dead skin, it seem to be reborn from its own death. The bull is also associated with the moon because of its crescent-shaped horns.

The sun is the second symbol of rebirth, which suggests a completely spiritual rebirth outside and beyond the field of space and time. The lion and eagle are associated with the sun. Combining the two sets of images, the lion pounces on the bull and the eagle pounces on the serpent. Campbell is stressing the idea that we experience rebirth here and now: by opening our awareness to how we exist both within and apart from the cycles of time. "That which you are was never born and will never die; that is the insight rendered in terms of the solar mystery, the solar light."[7]

The goal of many Asian religions is to bring us into accord with the "void which is no void," so we can realize our identity with the energy that seems to flow to us as experience.[8] In other words, time is the doorway and the barrier to our experience of the eternal self within. European traditions, on the other hand, separate humanity and the divine, and seek to bring about a relationship between the two.

Q: "You speak often of the shadows in time as in the symbolism of the moon. Is this the same as suffering in the midst of life?"[9]

Campbell answers this question by referencing the Cross of Christ and human marriage. Life is an inextricable mixture of agony and bliss, each feeding into the other in an alchemical process of becoming more human in the field of time. Gottfried von Strassburg sees this combination of pain and love in the image of Christ on the Cross. Campbell adds the battlefield and marriage as examples of difficult things that are worth the effort when undertaken for love. Marriage involves suffering because one is constantly sacrificing one's ego to the relationship. Out of the death of ego comes the reborn self, now in proper relationship to the Other, with all of the love and loss that this entails. The road to bliss travels through the heart of loss. This realization brings one through the valley of shadows and into the light of divine transformation.

Q: *"How does the ordinary person achieve transcendence and what role does ritual play in it?"*[10]

Campbell begins his response to this question by defining the term *transcendence*. One meaning of the word is the ability to go past, beyond, or outside of something. So a transcendent God can be imagined to exist beyond the world. But the other definition of *transcendence* is that which lies beyond conceptualization, beyond ideas. God, in this sense, is that which goes beyond all thinking, naming, and forms.

Campbell suggests that the ordinary person can experience transcendence through poetry and the arts. Creative work can open a door through which the experience happens.

Ritual can also create an experience of transcendence. When we reenact a myth, we might encounter the source of the myth directly, beyond concepts, names, and forms. Campbell elaborates on this idea by examining the rituals of initiation for boys and girls in traditional societies.

Q: *"The ritual seems to aim at the group. How does the individual participate?"*[11]

Campbell draws a distinction between two types of ritual in ancient Greece: local cults of city-states outside Athens that emphasized a communal, group experience, and the more literary festivals of classical Athens written for the individual viewer. He sees an overall lack of communal, myth-based ritual in America.

One example of the power of ritual is the Seder meal, which gives its participants a "strong sense of being a people together."[12]

"*Christ also said that man is not made for the Sabbath, but the Sabbath is made for man. In other words, the Law is to serve man and not man the Law.*"

—THOU ART THAT, *page 87*

Ritual can also be extremely dangerous, as in the case of the Nazi rallies that Hitler used to warp Germany's national consciousness.

Campbell sees effective ritual as well in the Catholic Mass, especially when celebrated in Latin, and in the contemporary picket line or protest line. In both these examples, the group comes together and identifies with something larger than their individual selves.

Q: "Would you enlarge on this idea of 'sacred space'?"[13]

Sacred space, according to Campbell, is set apart from secular activities and their many pairs of opposites "so that we may contemplate the unity and mystery revealed in all things."[14] Sacred spaces often contain many symbols and metaphors to help the community experience transcendence. Campbell offers the example of caves in France and Spain that contain symbolic paintings from tens of thousands of years ago.

In theory, all space is sacred space because all space is already infused with mystery and thus capable of transporting its occupants beyond the world of dualities. But before we can fully experience this, we must have first, according to Campbell, "learned the discipline of sacred space and appreciated the metaphoric significance of the objects found therein."[15]

Medieval cathedrals are excellent examples of sacred space. The architecture, art, and stained-glass windows are each awe-inspiring on their own. Together, they create an intense experience of the mythology that bound the society together.

Q: "You have referred in your work to the symbols of spiritual growth in the Kuṇḍalini yoga. Could you explain that briefly?"[16]

Campbell defines *Kuṇḍalini* as coiled up spiritual energy that rests at the base of the torso. Kuṇḍalini yoga is a focused practice of breathing and meditation that seeks to uncoil this energy and raise it through a succession of energetic centers along the spine called *cakras*: the genitals, navel, heart, throat, and spine.

Kuṇḍalini practitioners must be careful with this powerful energy until it reaches the level of the heart. Campbell sees the opening of the heart, cakra four, or love, as the remedy for aggression and lust. He cites Dante's feeling for Beatrice as love, and Acteon's gaze upon Artemis as lust. The first three cakras are the realm of "the human animal," but "the heart is the beginning of humanity."[17]

Campbell's goal in this section is to present the Kuṇḍalini system as an algorithm of progression from our base impulses, lust, anger, desire, loathing, into the "higher" states of compassion, love, awareness, knowledge, and wisdom. One progresses through these states through a program of "civilizing" the animal instincts and embracing the transformative power of meditation. The old adage that "you cannot fix a problem with the same thinking that caused the problem" looms large in this section.

Q: "Can you explore the notion of the Afterlife?"[18]

Many religious traditions speak of heavens and hells, where the dead experience a reflection of their experiences while they were alive. So those who spend their lives in anger, regret, selfishness, isolation, or resentment would experience those conditions after

death. Conversely, those who let go of their ego, open to the mystery of being, and become compassionate would experience that state. Christianity, Campbell points out, is the only tradition that sees Hell as a permanent state. Other traditions see hells as places to learn from and then leave.

Points of Interest

THE PROBLEM OF MYTHOLOGY IN OUR TIME

In this section, Campbell addresses obstacles to the proper understanding of myth: Literal interpretation renders most mythological symbols absurd, and Freudian interpretations reduce myth to a single psychological meaning. We end up with some people arguing myths refer to events that really happened, other people arguing that these events never happened, and others claiming that these symbols refer to repressed sexual trauma experienced by individuals before the advent of modern psychology. Campbell's interpretations encompass and go beyond all of these arguments. It is now up to us to find mythic symbols that activate the imagination and help us reconnect with the mystery out of which these symbols emerged.

THE SYMBOLISM OF REBIRTH

A mythological rebirth is an awakening of consciousness to the preconditions that are the basis of its own existence and form. In other words, we are born once into the world and then a second time into the realization that we are the world. And every time we further awaken to the ground of our being, individually and collectively, we are born again. And again. And again.

"When you realize that eternity is right here now, that it is within your possibility to experience the eternity of your own truth and being, then you grasp the following: That which you are was never born and will never die; that is the insight rendered in terms of the solar mystery, the solar light."

—THOU ART THAT, *page 90*

Chapter VII: Question Period

SACRED SPACE

Traditionally, communities would designate certain spaces to be sacred for the purposes of removing them from secular activities and concerns and reserving them for ritual, ceremony, worship, and other activities geared towards the transformation of consciousness. Whether those be existing spaces with special features in the landscape, or spaces created by the community for the purposes of conducting ritual and ceremony, sacred spaces are essential parts of spiritual experience and community building. Chosen by the community to represent the place of emergence, or that place where the veil is thinnest and the spirit is most likely to emerge and interact with the community, these spaces would then become the sites for the majority of the community's sacred rituals, traditions, and ceremonies. This tradition of claiming sacred space for the purposes of grounding and facilitating the sacred rites of the community goes back into the sacred caves of our Neolithic and Paleolithic ancestors.

Campbell understood that a symbolic encounter with a space allowed one to move beyond the world of opposites and experience the transcendence that is the ground of our being. He gives special attention to a place that nurtured his lifelong fascination with sacred space: Chartres Cathedral in France, a UNESCO World Heritage Site and considered by many to represent the high point in French Gothic art. The cathedral has changed very little since the fourteenth century, offering a window into the ways medieval Europeans conceived, articulated, and experienced sacred space. Campbell spent hundreds of hours under the flying buttresses of this medieval Gothic cathedral and nowhere else is his love for the mythic impulse more evident than when he is discusses sacred space such as Chartres.

Complementary Reading from Campbell's Work

Campbell, Joseph. *Reflections on the Art of Living: A Joseph Campbell Companion.* Harper Perennial, 1995.

—. *The Hero with a Thousand Faces.* Princeton University Press, 1973.

—. *Goddesses: Mysteries of the Feminine Divine.* New World Library, 2013.

Further Reading

Akomolafe, Bayo. *These Wilds Beyond Our Fences: Letters to My Daughter on Humanity's Search for Home.* North Atlantic Books, 2017.

Canon, Jon. *The Secret Language of Sacred Spaces: Decoding Churches, Cathedrals, Temples, Mosques and Other Places of Worship Around the World.* Watkins, 2013.

Eliade, Mircea. *The Sacred and The Profane: The Nature of Religion.* Harcourt Brace Jovanovich, 1987.

Galland, China. *Longing for Darkness: Tara and the Black Madonna.* Penguin, 2007.

Lawlor, Robert. *Sacred Geometry: Philosophy & Practice.* Thames & Hudson, 1982.

Ruck, Carl A.P. *Sacred Mushrooms: Secrets of Eleusis.* Ronin Publishing, 2006.

Chapter VII: Question Period

Discussion Questions

- In this chapter, Campbell addresses the importance of rituals in allowing the individual to develop transformative relationships to the Other. What role does ritual play in your life and how does it help you connect to community? To nature? To the divine?

- Campbell claims in this chapter that marriage should not be seen as a love affair but as an ordeal. What does he mean by this? Do you agree or disagree? Why?

- Campbell elaborates on the initiation rites for boys and girls in traditional societies that marked their transition from childhood into adulthood and, equally importantly, into their roles within the community. What are the kinds of initiatory rites that exist for young people today? Do you think they are effective in introducing them both to their own adult selves and to their place in the larger world?

- How and where do you encounter sacred space? How do you experience it?

Essay Topics

- Campbell speaks of the bull and the lion as symbolic animals for the moon and the sun, respectively. Write an essay tracing the development of these symbols across at least two mythological traditions.

"The battlefield is symbolic of the field of life in which all creatures survive because of the death of others. Thus we grasp the giving of oneself for whatever it is that is experienced as the object or value of one's love, the great example of which is Christ on the Cross."

—THOU ART THAT, *page 91*

- Have a conversation with a friend, relative, or colleague about what you have read in this book and see what questions they have about the motifs, themes, symbols, or metaphors discussed in the text. Write an essay researching one of their questions and share it with them.

- Campbell mentions in this chapter that "the earliest examples of sacred space are found in the caves in southern France and northern Spain, where extraordinary symbolic paintings were made 30,000 years ago."[19] Is this still true? Write a research essay about one (or more) of the sacred spaces we have discovered since Campbell made this statement.

- "I do not understand the idea of the Black Madonna,"[20] Campbell says in this chapter. Write a research essay where you try to help him understand it.

Creative Prompts

- Write a screenplay where you enter a dialogue with Campbell about the most important aspects of your own belief system. What questions would you ask him? How do you think he would respond? What questions might he ask you? How would you respond?

- Create a modern ritual of transformation. It can be based on an ancient or modern tradition but should be given a unique spin and meaning. Provide the steps of the ritual and its interpretation.

"Marriage, as I said, is not a love affair; it is an ordeal. If you think of it as that you will be able to go through with it. The ordeal consists specifically in sacrificing ego to the relationship."

—THOU ART THAT, *page 92*

- Develop a creative project (essay, short video, piece of art) that articulates what it is for you to enter and inhabit sacred space. Describe the space itself, how your consciousness changes when you are in it, and what benefits this brings to your life and relationships.

NOTES

1 Joseph Campbell, *Thou Art That*, 86.
2 Ibid, 87.
3 Ibid, 88.
4 Ibid, 89.
5 Ibid, 89.
6 Ibid, 89.
7 Ibid, 90.
8 Ibid, 90.
9 Ibid, 90.
10 Ibid, 92.
11 Ibid, 94.
12 Ibid, 95.
13 Ibid, 95.
14 Ibid, 95.
15 Ibid, 96.
16 Ibid, 98.
17 Ibid, 99.
18 Ibid, 100.
19 Ibid, 96.
20 Ibid, 97.

Appendix:
A Discussion

Chapter Summary

The final chapter in this collection is the transcription of an interview with Campbell that was originally published in the 1979 Easter edition of the *New York Times Magazine*. It was, according to Campbell, responsible for introducing more people to his work than any other interview he ever did. It was also the piece that introduced Campbell's work to Bill Moyers. It is, as the editor's note suggests, a fitting way to end this collection. In it, Campbell is in his finest form, evoking an ancient, fluid, strangely youthful and optimistic view of human potential as we continued into this new age of "no horizons."

We see Campbell here, as the interviewer recalls, as "Merlin standing with a pointer at the gates of the cosmos."[1] He summarizes the functions of myth, speaks about the mythological connections between Passover and Easter, and reflects on how the Space Age forces a reimagination of our place in the universe (and thus, our mythological systems as well).

Campbell discusses films like *Close Encounters of the Third Kind* and *2001: A Space Odyssey* as they relate to the myths of the moment and their symbolic aspects. He stresses the importance of symbolic interpretations of religious symbols and how that can revitalize religion. The conversation dwells on Campbell's interpretations of the religious and folk symbols of Easter and Passover and closes with Campbell's reflections on the importance of the *Earthrise* photograph as a contemporary mythic symbol.

Appendix: A Discussion

Points of Interest

THE SPACE AGE AND *EARTHRISE*

The symbolism and ample metaphors that spring from the conversation around the Space Age, and in particular the *Earthrise* image, really animate this entire conversation. Campbell was transfixed by the idea of humanity being able to look back at itself from the heavens via the image of the Earth and some of the Moon's surface that was taken from lunar orbit by astronaut William Anders on December 24, 1968, during the Apollo 8 mission. Nature photographer Galen Rowell described it as "the most influential environmental photograph ever taken," and Campbell seems to agree. He suggests in this part of the conversation that the Space Age has forced us to reevaluate all mythological symbols and narratives that previously placed the Earth at the center of the universe and put the heavens "up there" and the Earth "down here." The Earth sits in the heavens. There is no separation. And the new myths must be built, according to Campbell, upon the bedrock of this shifting perspective.

PASSOVER AND EASTER

The deeply resonant connections Campbell makes between the holidays of Passover and Easter stand as some of the finest observations of this chapter and a living testament to the importance of Campbell's work. Centuries of conflict between Jewish and Christian communities have obscured the fact that Judaism is the parent religion of Christianity and thus, many of the themes, motifs, metaphors, and transformative symbols within Christianity find their home in the mythological traditions of Judaism. But more to the point, each offers a glimpse at an older experience of transformation through rebirth. This is an archaic and ubiquitous symbol of the manner in which one engages the mythological traditions to ultimately move through them and into a direct relationship with the ground of their very being.

FLUIDITY OF VALUES AND IDENTITIES

In 2023, decades after Campbell's death, we are finally stepping fully into the fluid spaces of individual and communal identities that he somehow had the vision to mention were on the horizon in this chapter. The transition out of the old ways of knowing and being would open up spaces for humanity to realign itself within the complex web of life. Traditional categories of gender, race, religion, nationality, age, etc. would all become open to new avenues of association. Postmodernism, the literary, sociological, and philosophical response to the redundant and concretized definitions of modernity would eventually yield to a metamodern realignment, a new set of symbols, metaphors, and myths, which would carry the power to reintroduce the individual to the ancient and immediate ground of their being and becoming.

CRUCIFIXION AND RESURRECTION

Like his observation that both Passover and Easter are bound in a symbolic relationship that helps the individual transform and transcend the previous boundaries of an antiquated system of symbols and mythic narratives, his observation that there can be no resurrection without there first being a crucifixion is a vital, relevant contribution to what are often profoundly misunderstood aspects of the Christian story.

"There are no horizons in space, and there can be no horizons in our own experience. We cannot hold on to ourselves or our in-groups as we once did."

—THOU ART THAT, *page 104*

Complementary Reading from Campbell's Work

Campbell, Joseph. *The Power of Myth with Bill Moyers.* Anchor, 1991.

—. *The Hero's Journey: Joseph Campbell on His Life and Work.* New World Library, 2003.

—. *Pathways to Bliss: Mythology and Personal Transformation.* New World Library, 2004.

—. *The Flight of the Wild Gander: Explorations in the Mythological Dimension—Selected Essays 1944–1968.* New World Library, 2002.

—. *The Mythic Dimension: Selected Essays 1959–1987.* New World Library, 2017.

—. *Myths of Light: Eastern Metaphors of the Eternal.* New World Library, 2003.

Further Reading

Broom, Zachary. *Without God: Science, Belief, Morality, and the Meaning of Life.* Independently published, 2019.

Delio, Ilia. *Re-Enchanting the Earth: Why AI Needs Religion.* Orbis, 2020.

Haupt, Lyanda Lynn. *Rooted: Life at the Crossroads of Science, Nature, and Spirit.* Little, Brown Spark, 2023.

Kimmerer, Robin Wall. *Braiding Sweetgrass: Indigenous Wisdom, Scientific Knowledge and the Teachings of Plants.* Milkweed Editions, 2015.

Küng, Hans. *The Beginning of All Things: Science and Religion.* Wm. B. Eerdmans Publishing, 2008.

> "*Apocalypse does not point to a fiery Armageddon but to the fact that our ignorance and our complacency are coming to an end.*"
>
> —THOU ART THAT, *page 107*

Oliver, Kendrick. *To Touch the Face of God: The Sacred, the Profane, and the American Space Program, 1957–1975.* Johns Hopkins University Press, 2013.

Radin, Dean. *Real Magic: Ancient Wisdom, Modern Science, and a Guide to the Secret Power of the Universe.* Harmony, 2018.

Sacks, Jonathan. *The Great Partnership: Science, Religion, and the Search for Meaning.* Schocken, 2014.

Sagan, Carl. *The Varieties of Scientific Experience: A Personal View of the Search for God.* Penguin, 2007.

Slegers, Nathan. *Passover: The Story of Easter from the Beginning.* Come Thirsty Ministry, 2018.

Unger, Roberto Mangabeira. *The Religion of the Future.* Verso Books, 2016.

Winkler, Gershon. *Magic of the Ordinary: Recovering the Shamanic in Judaism.* North Atlantic Books, 2003.

Discussion Questions

- Campbell believed that the Space Age would fundamentally change the way we understood ourselves and the mythic symbols that had governed our religious institutions and spiritual thinking for millennia. Was he right? Why or why not?

- In what ways has the Internet Age continued to initiate the vast changes in mythological understanding and engagement that Campbell assumed would happen as a result of the Space Age?

Appendix: A Discussion

- Can the Earth still be considered the "center" of the universe? In other words, what does this mean metaphorically (for example, when we call someone we love the "center" of our world) and also from a literal perspective (in an infinite space, how is any point *not* the center)?

- At one point in this chapter Campbell asserts, "We hate ourselves so much that we take delight in the destruction of people."[2] Why does he say this is the case? Do you agree or disagree with him? Are there other reasons this might be true?

- Campbell claims that Passover and Easter are celebrations of transformation that should help us transcend the dead orthodoxy of outdated traditions and embrace the mysterious world of the now, the vibrant world of our continuous becoming. What do you make of this assertion? Are you aware of other traditions that seek to take the individual beyond even that which the tradition teaches is the highest good?

- Do you agree with the interviewer's assertion, based on Campbell's discussion of the tendency to read spiritual mythological symbols as though they were primarily references to historical events, that a re-mythologizing of the world would "rescue the stories of the Bible, then, from historical literalism and a susceptibility to debunking?"[3] How could this shift in perspective change the beliefs and practices of the religions that consider these texts sacred? How could that, in turn, change the world?

- At the time of this interview, in 1979, Campbell said that films like *Close Encounters of the Third Kind* and *2001: A Space Odyssey* were exactly the kinds of visual storytelling we needed to help us re-mythologize the world. What are some more modern examples of film, television, music, literature, or art that are accomplishing this today?

Essay Topics

- Write an essay exploring and developing the mythological and spiritual connections between Passover and Easter. Are there any other mythological celebrations that you can also connect to these two celebrations of spiritual transformation?

- Write an essay exploring the ways religious communities have tried to reinvigorate ancient myths to make them compatible with modern science and scholarship. Beyond a total rejection of modern science or a doubling down on orthodox positions, how are proponents of the "old religions" working to integrate their wisdom with the most modern and reliable scientific understandings of the cosmos?

- Write an essay researching a modern movement that is putting some of Campbell's observations into action, whether they realize it or not. Examples include meta-modernism, eco-psychology, Internal Family Systems, and narrative therapy.

"With our view of earthrise, we could see that the earth and the heavens were no longer divided but that the earth is in the heavens. There is no division and all theological notions based on the distinction between the heavens and the earth collapse with that realization."

—THOU ART THAT, *page 105-106*

"Through the Crucifixion we were unshelled, we were able to be born to resurrection. That is not a calamity. We must look freshly at this so that its symbolism can be sensed."

—THOU ART THAT, *page 112*

"The Kingdom of God is within us. Easter and Passover, particularly, remind us that we have to let go in order to enter it."

—THOU ART THAT, *page 114*

Appendix: A Discussion

Creative Prompts

- Write a creative script that is a fictional dialogue between Campbell and another personality of your choosing. Model it on the conversation in this chapter. Think about how you will present both characters in this mock interview and the questions and responses they will offer.

- Write a creative essay that examines how a species from another world might engage, interpret, and understand one of the mythological traditions of our world. Not being from Earth, what would feel alien to them? What might seem familiar to them, regardless of their place of origin?

- Create a piece of visual art and tell a story about it. The two, together, should help you, and us, re-mythologize the world.

NOTES

1 Joseph Campbell, *Thou Art That*, 114.
2 Ibid, 106.
3 Ibid, 111.

Final Thoughts
from Andrew Gurevich

I started writing this Skeleton Key Study Guide in early 2020, when the COVID-19 pandemic began its rampage across an unprepared and unsuspecting world. I sat in a hotel in Los Angeles with other members of the Joseph Campbell Foundation editorial team and watched news reports of a strange illness making people sick in Wuhan, China. A sickness that was starting to pop up in other places: London. Paris. Berlin. Seattle. New York. Miami. Los Angeles. None of us of could imagine what was coming next. I remember speaking with a hotel employee about this mysterious emerging sickness and the worrisome news that it was spreading so quickly. "Isn't that always the way it goes," he said. "Bad news always travels faster."

As I write the final lines of this study guide, roughly four years later, I still think about that conversation. Why does "bad news travel faster"? What is it about our species that relishes chaos, struggle, and division? Is it something about our biology? Is it culturally informed? Is it even true, or just a lingering perception rooted in something deeper about our complicated survival instincts? So much seems to have changed since that time. Today, we are facing years of "post-pandemic" recovery, an indicted former U.S. president, geopolitical instability, rising racial tensions and police brutality, the collapsing of longstanding global alliances and the establishing of new ones, massively destructive wildfires and hurricanes, and more uncertainty about our futures than ever before. And yet, the more things change, the more they stay the same. Something about our species is always struggling to find the balance between order and chaos. Conflict is intricately woven into the very fabric of our communal identities. And, it seems, it is from this conflict-riddled state that our collective future must emerge. But how? And when?

Campbell's life's work, and especially the teachings in *Thou Art That*, show us that there are many more pathways to reconciliation and a remembrance of our original inheritance coded into the world's wisdom traditions than many of us have realized. Even though we are at a time when the old mythologies no longer fully serve us, the seeds of a new beginning are rooting in the composting wisdom of that which came before. At the core of this organic reimagining of our collective mythos, we find that we must reconsider the traditional boundaries between self and other, between sacred and profane, and even between "enemy" and "ally."

Joseph Campbell will go down in history as one of the greatest integrationists of all time. His work reminds us that the ultimate battle is not so much against an external enemy, but rather against the ignorance, fear, and hatred that can prevail when we are not allowed, encouraged, or able to truly know ourselves. He opened doors that had been closed and bolted shut for several generations and invited us all to walk through them into a greater awareness of the spark of divinity that animates us all. In doing so, he also invited us to consider several of the underlying assumptions that have defined our experience and discussion of the sacred for most of the modern era.

A profound and vibrant wisdom emerges while reading *Thou Art That*, as we become conversant enough with the deep structures of our mythologies that they begin to speak to one another. This is a wisdom born from a return to mystery as a grounding principle that yields awe, humility, and gratitude. The conversational style of the text lends itself to guided discussions, dialogues, and group meditations. Is this the best way to teach myth? Perhaps.

The Upanishads came together as what became known as the "close-up" teachings. Hinduism had fallen into a chaotic conundrum of competing spiritual taxonomies, irreconcilable dogmas, murky histories, and ontological decadence. This was roughly during the same time that the Buddha sought Enlightenment through the era's decaying spiritual practices and found them all, for one reason or another, overpromising and underdelivering. So a new way of relating to the divine, and thus to one another, was born from the chaos. These "close-up" teachings required people to set aside their egoic proclamations and dogmatic assertions and speak directly to one another again. They encouraged listening, asking questions, meditating before responding, and becoming more comfortable with the ever-permeating reality of the mystery of our own existence and how we relate to the ground of our being.

We find ourselves in a similar place today.

My friend Nora Bateson, the daughter of the famed anthropologist Gregory Bateson, had this to say in a recent conversation: "To know that you live in a world in which you will change and be changed is to hold an idea of self gently enough to be reshaped, without breaking those around you. Every organism does this as seasons change. Life requires nothing less than infinite reshaping. This is grace."

Campbell gave me a grammar with which I could start to not only rebuild myself, but also build living bridges to others. I felt isolated and worthless because I was cut off from the fundamental awareness that I was never disconnected from anything. On the composting body of my trauma self, Campbell's words provided life-giving water to the emergence of something new. By remembering that I was already connected to everything, I was reminded that my individual self was, indeed, worthless in comparison to the vast, undifferentiated Oneness that was the ground of all being, knowledge, and forms. But in relationship to that Essence, I was something else altogether. I was also all of it. God was, and is, that which is not me, but also me. And from this vantage point I was able to relate to all things on the same level of awe, gratitude, and wonder.

I am Andrew Gurevich. For years, saying or writing this filled me with a sense of shame, or worse, emptiness. Now, because of so many moments of catharsis and transformation, not the least of which have been the works of Joseph Campbell, and this book in particular, I can say that when I write these words, "I am Andrew Gurevich," I am emptied of the limitations, negative projections, and sense of isolation that used to follow such a simple incantation. And instead, in the empty space that is exactly the size and shape of me, I am filled with the entire universe. For that I am grateful. For that I am humble. And for that I am hopeful.

Even as I write these final words, I am painfully aware of all this guide has left out. All of the brilliant authors, artists, creators, and thinkers I have not referenced. All of the great sample assignments and writing prompts I did not include. That's the trick, isn't it? We are always aware of what is missing when we try to encapsulate something as massive as the ideas contained in the pages of both Campbell's text and this companion

guide. To think otherwise would be to cut ourselves off from the ever-flowing fountain of divine wisdom, joy, being, and knowledge. When we are thirsty, we should drink and be satisfied, never forgetting the living water is there for us the next time we need to be replenished. If this study guide can accomplish anything of value, let it introduce the reader to the freedom and majesty of remaining incomplete. Let the reader emerge from this text filled with a desire to leave a seat at the table for the unexpected wonder of becoming.

"God is that which is not you, but also you." This simple algorithmic expression came to me in a dream during the creation of this guide. It is a distillation of so much of the core of what I believe Campbell devoted his life to exploring and expanding. It is a statement as true and authentically inhabited in the Hindu tradition as it is in the Judaic or Christian traditions. And as such, it is a key to unlocking so much of what it is to be a human in relationship to all that is, was, and will ever be. Campbell encouraged us to become transparent to transcendence, and he left us an inexhaustible trove of guides to help us manifest that sacred transparency in our own lives.

Thank you for going along for this ride. I hope at the end of this journey you will be able to see your reflection more clearly in all things, and thus welcome them into the multifaceted family of your mythical emergence.

About Joseph Campbell

Joseph Campbell was an American author and teacher best known for his work in the field of comparative mythology. He was born in New York City in 1904, and from early childhood he became interested in mythology. He loved to read books about Indigenous American cultures, and frequently visited the American Museum of Natural History in New York, where he was fascinated by the museum's collection of totem poles. Campbell was educated at Columbia University, where he specialized in medieval literature, and, after earning a master's degree, continued his studies at universities in Paris and Munich. While abroad he was influenced by the art of Pablo Picasso and Henri Matisse, the novels of James Joyce and Thomas Mann, and the psychological studies of Sigmund Freud and Carl Jung. These encounters led to Campbell's theory that all myths and epics are linked in the human psyche, and that they are cultural manifestations of the need to explain social, cosmological, and spiritual realities.

After a period in California, where he encountered John Steinbeck and the biologist Ed Ricketts, Campbell taught at the Canterbury School, and then, in 1934, joined the literature department at Sarah Lawrence College, a post he retained for many years. During the 1940s and '50s, he helped Swami Nikhilananda to translate the Upaniṣads and *The Gospel of Sri Ramakrishna*. He also edited works by the German scholar Heinrich Zimmer on Indian art, myths, and philosophy. In 1944, with Henry Morton Robinson, Campbell published *A Skeleton Key to Finnegans Wake*. His first original work, *The Hero with a Thousand Faces*, came out in 1949 and was immediately well received; in time, it became acclaimed as a classic. In this study of the "myth of the hero," Campbell asserted that there is a single pattern of heroic journey and that all cultures share this essential pattern in their various heroic myths. In his book he also outlined the basic conditions, stages, and results of the archetypal hero's journey.

Joseph Campbell died in 1987. In 1988, a series of television interviews with Bill Moyers, *The Power of Myth*, introduced Campbell's views to millions of people.

About the Author

Andrew Gurevich is a professor of mythology, religion, and ancient literature. He is the former president of the Association for the Anthropology of Consciousness, an academic organization that studies anthropological approaches to understanding consciousness, and is a member of the Editorial Advisory Board for the Joseph Campbell Foundation. Andrew lives in Portland, Oregon, with his wife and two children. He is the author of numerous rhetorical artifacts that explore the living presence of the sacred in the human story.

About the Joseph Campbell Foundation

The Joseph Campbell Foundation invites you to experience the power of myth. Building on the work of Joseph Campbell, we offer resources and community for those who hear the call to adventure.

For more information about Joseph Campbell and the Joseph Campbell Foundation, contact:

Joseph Campbell Foundation
www.jcf.org

www.ingramcontent.com/pod-product-compliance
Lightning Source LLC
Chambersburg PA
CBHW061807070526
44586CB00024B/2754